CRAC 2022 Shared Task on Multilingual Coreference Resolution

AA004824

Gyeongju, South Korea
17 October 2022

ISBN: 978-1-7138-9089-8

Printed from e-media with permission by:

Curran Associates, Inc.
57 Morehouse Lane
Red Hook, NY 12571

Some format issues inherent in the e-media version may also appear in this print version.

Copyright© (2022) by the Association for Computational Linguistics and the authors.
All rights reserved.

Printed with permission by Curran Associates, Inc. (2024)

For permission requests, please contact the Association for Computational Linguistics at the address below.

Association for Computational Linguistics
209 N. Eighth Street
Stroudsburg, Pennsylvania 18360

Phone: 1-570-476-8006
Fax: 1-570-476-0860

acl@aclweb.org

Additional copies of this publication are available from:

Curran Associates, Inc.
57 Morehouse Lane
Red Hook, NY 12571 USA
Phone: 845-758-0400
Fax: 845-758-2633
Email: curran@proceedings.com
Web: www.proceedings.com

COLING

International Conference on Computational Linguistics

Proceedings of the Conference and Workshops

COLING

Volume 29 (2022), No. 21

Proceedings of the CRAC 2022 Shared Task on Multilingual Coreference Resolution

The 29th International Conference on Computational Linguistics

October 17, 2022
Gyeongju, Republic of Korea

Copyright of each paper stays with the respective authors (or their employers).

ISSN 2951-2093

Message from the Program Chairs

This volume contains papers describing the CRAC 2022 Shared Task on Multilingual Coreference Resolution and the participating systems. The public edition of the multilingual collection CorefUD 1.0 was used as the source of training and evaluation data, spanning 13 datasets for 10 languages, namely Catalan, Czech, English, French, German, Hungarian, Lithuanian, Polish, Russian, and Spanish. Shared task participants were supposed to identify mentions in texts and to predict coreference relations between the identified mentions; only identity coreference is considered in this shared task.

A total of 5 teams participated in this task, with 8 submitted systems ranging from a very simple rule-based system to a deep-learning system trained jointly on all languages. In this volume, system description papers delivered by 3 teams are presented, preceded with an overview paper describing in more detail the task itself, the input data, the baseline system, the main evaluation metric, and global performance comparisons.

From our viewpoint, major goals of the shared task were reached: not only that new systems capable of coreference resolution in various languages were created, but the state-of-the-art performance for the given multilingual collection was improved considerably. We hope that this success will attract new researchers to the area of multilingual coreference resolution, and hopefully also new participants to the future editions of the present shared task.

We would like to thank all the participants for their efforts, and program committee members for reviewing the submitted manuscripts. Last but not least, we would like to thank organizers of the previous shared tasks for sharing their experience with us, and in general all authors of the involved coreference datasets for making the results of their work publicly accessible.

September 2022
Maciej Ogrodniczuk, Zdeněk Žabokrtský
on behalf of the shared task organizers

Shared task specification

https://ufal.mff.cuni.cz/corefud/crac22

Shared task organizers

- Charles University (Prague, Czechia):
  - Anna Nedoluzhko
  - Michal Novák
  - Martin Popel
  - Zdeněk Žabokrtský
  - Daniel Zeman
- Institute of Computer Science, Polish Academy of Sciences (Warsaw, Poland):
  - Maciej Ogrodniczuk
- Georgetown University (Washington D.C., USA):
  - Yilun Zhu
- University of West Bohemia (Pilsen, Czechia):
  - Miloslav Konopík
  - Ondřej Pražák
  - Jakub Sido

Program Committee

- Haixia Chai
- Christian Hardmeier
- Veronique Hoste
- Loic De Langhe
- Ekaterina Lapshinova-Koltunski
- Yaqin Yang
- Juntao Yu
- Yilun Zhu

Table of Contents

CRAC Shared Task session program

Monday, October 17, 2022

09:00–10:30 Shared Task papers

09:00–09:30 *Findings of the Shared Task on Multilingual Coreference Resolution*
Zdeněk Žabokrtský, Miloslav Konopík, Anna Nedoluzhko, Michal Novák, Maciej Ogrodniczuk, Martin Popel, Ondřej Pražák, Jakub Sido, Daniel Zeman and Yilun Zhu

09:30–09:45 *Coreference Resolution for Polish: Improvements within the CRAC 2022 Shared Task*
Karol Saputa

09:45–10:00 *End-to-end Multilingual Coreference Resolution with Mention Head Prediction*
Ondřej Pražák and Miloslav Konopik

10:00–10:15 *ÚFAL CorPipe at CRAC 2022: Effectivity of Multilingual Models for Coreference Resolution*
Milan Straka and Jana Straková

10:15–10:30 *Discussion*

10:30–11:00 Coffee Break

11:00–12:00 Invited Talk

11:00–12:00 *The recent developments in Universal Anaphora Scorer*
Juntao Yu

Findings of the Shared Task on Multilingual Coreference Resolution

Zdeněk Žabokrtský[1], Miloslav Konopík[2], Anna Nedoluzhko[1], Michal Novák[1], Maciej Ogrodniczuk[3], Martin Popel[1], Ondřej Pražák[2], Jakub Sido[2], Daniel Zeman[1], Yilun Zhu[4]

[1] Charles University, Faculty of Mathematics and Physics,
Institute of Formal and Applied Linguistics, Prague, Czechia
{zabokrtsky,nedoluzhko,mnovak,popel,zeman}@ufal.mff.cuni.cz

[2] University of West Bohemia, Faculty of Applied Sciences,
Department of Computer Science and Engineering, Pilsen, Czechia
konopik@kiv.zcu.cz, {ondfa,sidoj}@ntis.zcu.cz

[3] Institute of Computer Science, Polish Academy of Sciences
Warsaw, Poland, maciej.ogrodniczuk@gmail.com

[4] Georgetown University, Department of Linguistics,
Washington, DC, USA, yz565@georgetown.edu

Abstract

This paper presents an overview of the shared task on multilingual coreference resolution associated with the CRAC 2022 workshop. Shared task participants were supposed to develop trainable systems capable of identifying mentions and clustering them according to identity coreference. The public edition of CorefUD 1.0, which contains 13 datasets for 10 languages, was used as the source of training and evaluation data. The CoNLL score used in previous coreference-oriented shared tasks was used as the main evaluation metric. There were 8 coreference prediction systems submitted by 5 participating teams; in addition, there was a competitive Transformer-based baseline system provided by the organizers at the beginning of the shared task. The winner system outperformed the baseline by 12 percentage points (in terms of the CoNLL scores averaged across all datasets for individual languages).

1 Introduction

Multilingual shared tasks are an important source of momentum in various subfields of NLP research, with the CoNLL-X shared task on multilingual dependency parsing (Buchholz and Marsi, 2006) being one of the most successful and influential examples. Clearly, the limiting factor for organizing such shared tasks is the availability of multilingual data whose annotations are harmonized at least to some extent, so that the experiments on individual languages can be performed and evaluated in a uniform way.

In the coreference world, one of the first multilingual shared tasks were SemEval-2010 (Recasens et al., 2010) with seven languages and CoNLL-2012 (Pradhan et al., 2012), in which OntoNotes data for three languages (English, Chinese, and Arabic) were included. With the recent advance of the CorefUD collection (Nedoluzhko et al., 2021a, 2022), harmonized coreference data for 10 languages (covered in CorefUD's publicly available edition) became available. Hence, CorefUD is the source of data for the present shared task; more information about the collection is given in Section 2. In brief, participants of this shared task are supposed to (a) identify mentions in texts and (b) predict which mentions belong to the same coreference cluster (i.e., refer to the same entity or event), using the CorefUD data both for training and evaluation of their coreference resolution systems.

A specific feature of CorefUD is that it combines coreference with dependency syntax, using the annotation scheme (and file format too) of the Universal Dependencies (UD) project (de Marneffe et al., 2021). In all datasets included in the collection, the coreference annotation is manual and the dependency annotation is either manual too, if available, or produced by a dependency parser. Empirical evidence showing advantages of such symbiosis of coreference and dependency syntax is presented in two case studies (Popel et al., 2021; Nedoluzhko et al., 2021b). Participants of this shared task can employ the dependency annotation for determining mention spans (as mentions often correspond to syntactically meaningful units) and for determining core parts of mentions (which correspond to syntactic head in CorefUD).

To the best of our knowledge, this is the first

Proceedings of the CRAC 2022 Shared Task on Multilingual Coreference Resolution, pages 1–17
October 17, 2022

shared task on multilingual coreference resolution that accepts zeros (e.g. elided subjects) as potential members of coreference chains.[1] Zeros are an integral part of some of the CorefUD datasets, using empty nodes in enhanced UD representation to annotate them. We keep all annotated zeros, encouraging participants to resolve coreference also for this type of potential mentions.

As with other shared tasks, evaluation is crucial. Unfortunately, and unlike e.g. in dependency parsing, there is no simple and easily interpretable accuracy metric for coreference. We adhere to using the CoNLL score developed in former coreference shared tasks. More specifically, we use an average of the F_1 values of MUC, B^3 and CEAF-e scores as the main evaluation metric. More details concerning evaluation are presented in Section 3.

A Transformer-based coreference prediction system (Pražák et al., 2021) was provided as a strong baseline to the shared task participants. The baseline system as well as 8 systems submitted by the participants are briefly described in Section 4 and some of the systems are described in more detail in separate papers in this volume. Their results are summarized in Section 5. Possible directions for future editions of the shared task are outlined in Section 6.

2 Datasets

For training and evaluation purposes, the present shared task uses 13 coreference datasets for 10 languages as available in the public edition of the CorefUD 1.0 collection (Nedoluzhko et al., 2022) and follows the train/dev/test split of the collection, too.

2.1 Data Resources

Key features of the original coreference resources harmonized under the CorefUD scheme are extracted from Nedoluzhko et al. (2022) into the following paragraphs; some of their quantitative properties are summarized in Table 1.

Prague Dependency Treebank (Czech) (denoted as cs_pdt for short in this paper) is a corpus of Czech newspaper texts (~830K tokens) with manual multi-layer annotation (Hajič et al., 2020). Coreference and bridging relations are annotated as links on the deep syntactic layer. The links lead from the node of the syntactic head of the anaphor to the node representing the syntactic head of the antecedent and the whole subtrees of these nodes are considered to be mention spans.

Prague Czech-English Dependency Treebank – the Czech part (cs_pcedt) is one side of the PCEDT parallel corpus (Nedoluzhko et al., 2016) consisting of more than 1M tokens. The annotation of coreference-like phenomena is principally similar to the Prague Dependency Treebank with some minor differences and no bridging annotation.

Georgetown University Multilayer Corpus (English) (en_gum) (Zeldes, 2017) is a growing open source corpus of 12 written and spoken English genres (~180K tokens as of 2022). Next to UD syntax trees and discourse parses, it exhaustively annotates all mentions, including nested, named/non-named entities, singletons, and 10 entity classes and 6 information status tags. It distinguishes 8 anaphoric links: pronominal anaphora and cataphora, lexical and predicative coreference, apposition, discourse deixis, split antecedents and bridging. For licence reasons, Reddit data is excluded from both the UD_English-GUM and CorefUD 1.0 releases of GUM.

Polish Coreference Corpus (pl_pcc) (Ogrodniczuk et al., 2013, 2015) is a corpus (~ 540K tokens) of Polish nominal coreference built upon the National Corpus of Polish (Przepiórkowski et al., 2008). Mentions are annotated as linear spans, with additionally marked semantic heads. The annotation includes identity coreference, quasi-identity relations and non-identity close-to-coreference relations.

Democrat (French) (fr_democrat) (Landragin, 2021) is a diachronic corpus of written French texts from the 12th to the 21st century. The annotation focuses on nominal mentions (pronouns and full NPs only) and includes information of definiteness and syntactic type of mentions. Its conversion in CorefUD is based only on its automatically parsed subset of texts from 19th-21st century (Wilkens et al., 2020) (~280K tokens).

Russian Coreference Corpus (ru_rucor) (Toldova et al., 2014) is a corpus of ~150K tokens annotated with anaphoric and coreferential relations between noun groups. Mentions are annotated as linear spans, with additionally

[1] Recasens et al. (2010) do not state how zeros were treated for pro-drop languages such as Spanish and Catalan in SemEval-2010, and Pradhan et al. (2012) excluded all zeros from the CoNLL-2012 shared task data.

CorefUD dataset	docs	sents	words	zeros	entities	avg. len.	non-singletons
Catalan-AnCora	1550	16,678	546,665	6,377	69,239	1.6	62,416
Czech-PCEDT	2312	49,208	1,155,755	43,054	52,743	3.4	178,376
Czech-PDT	3165	49,428	834,721	32,617	78,880	2.5	169,545
English-GUM	175	9,130	164,392	92	24,801	1.9	28,054
English-ParCorFull	19	543	10,798	0	180	4.0	718
French-Democrat	126	13,054	284,823	0	40,937	2.0	47,172
German-ParCorFull	19	543	10,602	0	259	3.5	896
German-PotsdamCC	176	2,238	33,222	0	3,752	1.4	2,519
Hungarian-SzegedKoref	400	8,820	123,968	4,857	5,182	3.0	15,165
Lithuanian-LCC	100	1,714	37,014	0	1,224	3.7	4,337
Polish-PCC	1828	35,874	538,885	470	127,688	1.5	82,804
Russian-RuCor	181	9,035	156,636	0	3,636	4.5	16,193
Spanish-AnCora	1635	17,662	559,782	8,112	73,210	1.7	70,664

Table 1: Data sizes in terms of the total number of documents, sentences, tokens, zeros (empty words), coreference entities, average entity length (in number of mentions) and the total number of non-singleton mentions. Train/dev/test splits of these datasets roughly follow 8/1/1 ratio. See Nedoluzhko et al. (2022) for details.

distinguished syntactic heads. Only NPs which take part in coreference relations are considered and singletons are not annotated.

ParCorFull (German and English) (de_parcorfull and en_parcorfull) is a parallel corpus of ~160K tokens annotated for coreference (Lapshinova-Koltunski et al., 2018). Mentions are NPs which form part of pronoun-antecedent pairs, pronouns without antecedents or VPs if they are antecedents of anaphoric NPs (discourse deixis). The annotation includes identity coreference relations only. Due to license restrictions, CorefUD contains only its WMT News section (~20K tokens).

AnCora: Multi-level Annotated Corpora for Catalan and Spanish (ca_ancora and es_ancora) (Taulé et al., 2008; Recasens and Martí, 2010) consist of very detailed annotations of coreference (including zero anaphora, split antecedent, discourse deixis, etc.). The corpora (~1M tokens) also contain annotations of related phenomena such as argument structure, thematic roles, semantic classes of verbs, named entities, denotative types of deverbal nouns etc.

Potsdam Commentary Corpus (German) (de_potsdam) is a relatively small (~35K tokens) corpus of newspaper articles (Bourgonje and Stede, 2020) annotated for nominal and pronominal identity coreference. Mentions are further classified into primary (e.g. pronouns, definite NPs, proper names), secondary (indefinite NPs, clauses), and non-referring mentions. The corpus also contains gold constituent syntax, information structure (including topic and focus, see Lüdeling et al. (2016)), and discourse parses.

Lithuanian Coreference Corpus (lt_lcc) (Žitkus and Butkienė, 2018) is a corpus of written texts, focusing on political news (~35K tokens). Coreference annotation is link-based and additional coreference information is divided into four levels that include types of mentions, types of anaphoric relations, the direction of the relation, and annotation of split antecedents.

SzegedKoref: Hungarian Coreference Corpus (hu_szeged) (Vincze et al., 2018) is a corpus of written texts (~125K tokens) selected from the Szeged Treebank. The treebank has manual annotations at several linguistic layers such as deep phrase-structured syntactic analysis, dependency syntax and morphology. Mentions are linear spans without specially marked heads, the relations are classified into anaphoric classes such as repetitions, synonyms, hypernyms, hyponyms etc.

2.2 Annotation Details

CorefUD collection is fully compliant with the CoNLL-U format,[2] using the MISC column for annotation of coreference. Besides coreference,

[2]`https://universaldependencies.org/format.html`

also other anaphoric relations (e.g. bridging, split antecedents) are labeled in some CorefUD datasets. Nevertheless, the shared task focuses only on coreference. Therefore, the participants are asked to predict only the Entity attribute in the MISC column, namely the bracketing of mention spans (including possible discontinuities) and entity/cluster IDs assigning the mentions to entities. They do not need to identify mention heads or fill other coreference-related features that can be found in CorefUD data.

Reconstructed zeros are an integral part of some of the CorefUD datasets. CorefUD utilizes empty nodes in enhanced UD representation to mark them. In the shared task data, we keep all annotated zeros and ask the participants to predict coreference also for them. However, note that we decided not to strip off the empty nodes from the test data in the first edition of the shared task. Although some datasets mark also non-anaphoric zeros, presence of an empty node may indicate its anaphoricity. Its assignment to a cluster of other mentions still remains unknown, yet this makes the setup a bit unrealistic. We find it a reasonable compromise between exploring insufficiently known area of zero anaphora in coreference resolution and making the shared task simple and accessible.

Apart from annotation of coreference and anaphora, CorefUD comprises also standard UD-like annotation of parts of speech, morphological features and dependency syntax. With some exceptions, if the original resources contained manual annotation of morpho-syntax, it has been kept also in CorefUD. Otherwise, it has been obtained automatically using UDPipe 2.0 (Straka, 2018). Therefore, it must be noted that if a system takes advantage of this morpho-syntactic information, its performance on the datasets with manual morpho-syntax may be a bit overestimated, compared to real-world NLP scenarios in which manual annotations of morphology and syntax are usually not available.

3 Evaluation Metrics

Systems participating in the shared task are evaluated with the CorefUD scorer.[3] The primary evaluation score is the CoNLL F_1 score with singletons excluded and using partial mention matching. We also assess the shared task submissions by multiple supplementary scores.

[3]https://github.com/ufal/corefud-scorer

Official scorer We use our modification of the coreference scorer – CorefUD scorer. It is based on the Universal Anaphora (UA) scorer (Yu et al., 2022)[4] reusing the implementations of all generally used coreferential measures without any modification. This guarantees that the measures are computed in exactly the same way. However, our scorer is capable of processing the coreference annotation files in the CorefUD 1.0 format. Among other things, it allows evaluation of coreference for zeros.[5] Moreover, it re-defines matching of key and response mentions in the way to be able to handle potentially discontinuous mentions, which are present in some CorefUD datasets. Last but not least, we proposed and implemented the MM score to measure the accuracy of mention matching (see below).

Partial matching The CorefUD collection includes datasets (e.g. cs_pdt) that do not specify mention spans in their original annotations. In these datasets, a mention is only specified by its head and loosely by a dependency subtree rooted in this head. Also in other datasets, the exact specification of mention boundaries may be difficult, for instance, if mentions comprise embedded clauses, long detailed specifications, etc. Therefore, authors of some datasets address this issue by defining a syntactic or semantic head (single word) or a minimal span (multiple words possible, e.g. in ARRAU, Uryupina et al., 2020), i.e., a unit that carries the most important semantic information.

CorefUD specifies a mention head only syntactically. However, as it has been shown in Nedoluzhko et al. (2021b), heads labeled within coreference annotation most often correspond to heads defined by a dependency tree.

Availability of heads/minimal spans in key (i.e. gold reference) annotation allows for *partial mention matching* during the computation of any evaluation measure. In the UA scorer, a response (i.e. predicted by a system) mention matches a key mention if the boundaries of the response span lie within the key span and surround the key minimal span at the same time. In order to support evaluation of discontinuous mentions, we modified this criterion using a set/subset relation. In the

[4]This in turn reimplements the official CoNLL-2012 scorer (Pradhan et al., 2014).

[5]Nonetheless, the current implementation is not able to handle a response document whose tokens are not completely identical to ones in the key document. This holds also for empty nodes.

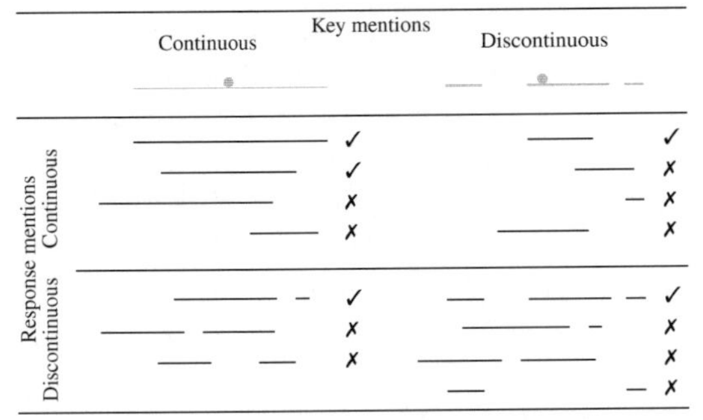

Figure 1: Examples of successful and unsuccessful partial mention matching of key mentions (the yellow ones in the top; the mention head depicted by a small circle) by various response mentions. Showing cases of both continuous and discontinuous mentions. Recall the definition of partial match: A response mention matches a key mention if all its words are included in the key mention and one of them is the key head.

CorefUD scorer, a response mention matches a key mention if all its words are included in the key mention and one of them is the key head. See Figure 1 for examples of response mentions that succeed or fail to match a key mention, depending on whether the mentions are continuous or discontinuous.

Head matching The *partial-match* approach to evaluation described above has two disadvantages. First, it suffices for the systems to predict only heads instead of full mention spans. For this reason, we report also the *exact-match* version as a secondary measure.

Second, some authors may decide to post-process predictions of their systems by reducing the span of each mention to the head word only using one of the methods described below. We can see in Table 4 that five systems (*straka*, berulasek and simple-rule-based*) applied this post-processing and improved thus their results in terms of the primary metric. However, this post-processing can be applied to any system, so we have decided to introduce it as another secondary metric called *head-match*. This way we can see what is the effect of such post-processing for systems which have not applied it. The *head-match* metric is even more benevolent than *partial-match* because it does not penalize extra words added to the span as long as the head remains the same.

The shared task did not require to predict the head in each mention. However, the head can be predicted given the span and the provided dependency tree as the "highest" node. We used Udapi block `corefud.MoveHead` for this purpose.[6]

The easiest post-processing method (chosen in all three *straka** submissions) is to reduce the span of each mention to the head.[7] However, the resulting CoNLL-U files may be invalid because two mentions may be assigned the same span.[8] One solution (chosen in the *berulasek* submission) is to merge the entities of the two mentions which got assigned the same span. In the *head-match* solution, we chose a more conservative solution: if two spans share the same head, we reduce only the smaller span and keep the larger span intact. We confirmed that differences between the three methods described in this paragraph according to the evaluation metrics are negligible because the cases of two mentions sharing the same head are rare.

Singletons The primary score is calculated excluding potential singletons, i.e., entities comprising only a single mention, in both key and response coreference chains. We selected this option as the primary metric because a majority of datasets in the CorefUD collection does not have singletons annotated.

Primary score As a primary evaluation metric, we employed the CoNLL F_1 score (Denis and Baldridge, 2009; Pradhan et al., 2014), which has been established as a standard for the evaluation of coreference resolution. It is an unweighted average of F_1 scores of three coreference measures: MUC (Vilain et al., 1995), B^3 (Bagga and Baldwin, 1998) and CEAF-e (Luo, 2005), each adopting a different view on coreference relations, namely link-based, mention-based and entity-based, respectively. A single primary score providing a final ranking of participating submissions is a macro-average over all datasets in the CorefUD test collection.

Supplementary scores In addition to the primary CoNLL F_1 score, we calculate three alternative

[6] `https://github.com/udapi/udapi-python/blob/master/udapi/block/corefud/movehead.py` This block was used also for annotating the heads in the gold data.

[7] With Udapi, it can be done using a command `udapy -s corefud.MoveHead util.Eval coref_mention='mention.words=[mention.head]' < in.conllu > out.conllu`.

[8] For example in coordinations, the mention covering the whole coordination and the mention covering the first conjunct share the same head. It should be noted we did not require the submissions to pass the official UD validation tests (`validate.py --level 2 --coref`).

versions of this metric: head-match, exact-match and with-singletons.

Besides the primary score and its three variants, we also report the systems' performance in terms of two additional scores: BLANC (Recasens and Hovy, 2011) and LEA (Moosavi and Strube, 2016).

In addition, we implement the MOR[9] score measuring to what extent key and response mentions match, no matter to which coreference entity they belong. First, we find such one-to-one alignment $A(\mathcal{K}, \mathcal{R})$ between the sets of all key mentions $\mathcal{K}$ and all response mentions $\mathcal{R}$ that maximizes the overall number of overlapping words within aligned mentions. We then calculate the recall of mention overlap as a ratio of the total number of overlapping words in mentions and the overall size of all key mentions (sum of its lengths):

$$MOR_{rec} = \frac{\sum_{(K,R) \in A(\mathcal{K},\mathcal{R})} |K \cap R|}{\sum_{K \in \mathcal{K}} |K|}$$

Precision is calculated analogously using the set of all response mentions $\mathcal{R}$ in the denominator. Note that position of the head in mentions does not play a role in MOR score.

In order to show performance of the systems on zeros, we use an anaphor-decomposable score which is an application of the scoring schema introduced by Tuggener (2014). For each zero mention other than the first one in the entity, we indicate a *true positive (tp)* case if an overlap in at least one preceding mention is found between respective key and response entities. *Wrong linkage (wl)* is indicated if no such mention is found and *False positive/negative (fp/fn)* case if the anaphoric response/key mention is not anaphoric (or it is the first mention of the entity) in the key/response document, respectively. Having these counts aggregated, recall is calculated as $\frac{tp}{tp+wl+fn}$ and precision as $\frac{tp}{tp+wl+fp}$.

4 Participating Systems

4.1 Baseline

The baseline system (BASELINE[10]) is based on the multilingual coreference resolution system presented by Pražák et al. (2021). The model uses multilingual BERT (Devlin et al., 2018) in the end-to-end setting. In high-level terms, the model goes through all potential spans and maximizes the probability of gold antecedents for each span. The same system is used for all the languages in the training dataset.

The simplified system adapted to CorefUD 1.0 is publicly available on GitHub[11] along with tagged dev data and its dev data results.

4.2 System Comparison

Table 2 shows the basic properties of all submitted systems for evaluation. The table is organized by individual teams. Some teams submitted more than one system. Roughly half of the systems exploited the provided baseline and the majority of the systems relied on machine learning.

Further details of the machine learning systems are described in Table 3. The table indicates that all machine-learning systems rely on large pretrained models consisting of hundreds of millions of parameters. The ÚFAL CorPipe team and the UWB team employ multilingual models. Karol Saputa utilizes a Polish model as he submitted results for Polish only. All teams who developed their deep-learning solution use the maximum sequence length of 512 sub-word tokens which equals the maximum allowed length of the employed models. Clearly, all the teams are aware of the necessity to model long dependencies in the coreference resolution task. The ÚFAL CorPipe trains on sentences and they put 8 samples in a batch. The UWB team works with documents and they put 1 document in a batch. Karol Saputa uses a dynamic batch to fill the buffer of 4 000 subwords. The number of gradient updates is similar to the teams that train on all languages. Karol Saputa trains with a much smaller number of updates since he trains only on one corpus.

4.3 Teams

The descriptions below are based on the information provided by the respective participants in an online questionnaire.

ÚFAL CorPipe submitted three systems (for details see (Straka and Straková, 2022) in this volume). All are based on pre-trained masked language models, either the RemBERT (Chung et al., 2020) or the XLM-RoBERTa (Conneau et al., 2019) large models. Each sentence is processed as an individual example. Additionally, the neighboring sentences from the document are included

[9] It stands for Mention Overlap Ratio.

[10] The baseline system was submitted to CodaLab under the name *sidoj*, but we rename it here to BASELINE for clarity.

[11] https://github.com/ondfa/coref-multiling

Team	Submission	Baseline based	Approach
ÚFAL CorPipe	straka	No	DL
	straka-single-multilingual-model	No	DL
	straka-only-single-treebank-data	No	DL
UWB	ondfa	Yes	DL
	BASELINE	–	DL
Matouš Moravec	Moravec	Yes – files only	rule-based postprocess of DL
Barbora Dohnalová	berulasek	Yes – files only	rule-based postprocess of DL
	simple-rule-based	No	rules
Karol Saputa	k-sap	No	DL

Table 2: System comparison. The baseline solution, if involved, was either modified internally, or only its predictions were used and modified subsequently ("files only"). "DL" stands for a deep learning solution.

Team	Submission	Model	SL	Size	Batch size	Updates	HParams
ÚFAL CorPipe	straka	google/rembert	512	614M	8	960k	4
	straka-single...	google/rembert	512	614M	8	960k	4
	straka-only...	google/rembert	512	614M	8	960k	4
UWB	ondfa	xlm-roberta-large	512	600M	1	800k	4
	BASELINE	multiling. BERT	512	220M	1	800k	0
Karol Saputa	k-sap	allegro/herbert-base-cased	512	415M	Dynamic	27k	$\sim$10

Table 3: Machine Learning Parameters. SL means sequence length, Size is the number of trainable parameters in the models, Updates is the number of gradient updates during training and HParames shows the number of tuned hyper-parameters.

as context – the right context is limited to 50 subwords, and the size of the left context is chosen so that the whole input has 512 subwords. The model is trained jointly to perform two tasks – mention span detection and coreference linking. The mention detection is trained using a CRF sequence tagging scheme based on a generalization of BIO encoding allowing overlapping mentions. Then, for each mention, it is decided which of the preceding mentions is its antecedent (selecting the original mention if there is no antecedent). To obtain a distribution over the previous mentions, a query and a key are computed using a nonlinear transformation, and then masked dot-product attention is utilized. Some experiments include *corpus id* – a special token at the beginning of a sample indicating the source corpus of the sample.

The *straka* system is trained jointly on all training data in all languages. This strategy exhibited a considerably better performance than training on individual corpora separately. For each corpus, the optimal model and epoch is chosen according to its development score. The *straka-single-multilingual-model* system employs a single checkpoint of a single model, thus corresponding to a real deployment scenario. The chosen model is based on Rembert, samples training data according to the logarithm of the respective corpus size, and does not utilize the corpus id. The *straka-only-single-treebank-data* system uses an independent model for each corpus with corresponding training data only. The model is based on Rembert, and for each corpus the submitted predictions are from the epoch with the best development performance. All three submissions were post-processed by reducing mentions spans to the head (cf. Head matching in Section 3).

UWB submitted one system *ondfa* which extends the baseline system (for details see Pražák and Konopik (2022) in this volume). The system relies on combined datasets to employ cross-lingual training. The authors did not know the exact procedure to generate heads for mentions. Therefore, they attempted to learn the heads from the data. The system relies on XLM-Roberta large, which is a substantially bigger model than in the baseline.

Barbora Dohnalová submitted two systems, *berulasek* and *simple-rule-based*, implemented as rule-based blocks in Udapi (Popel et al., 2017).[12]

berulasek post-processes the baseline predictions by first reducing mention spans to the head (cf. Head matching in Section 3) and then adding all proper nouns (upos=PROPN) with the same lemma into the same entity cluster (potentially adding new mentions to existing entities). The second step is applied only to cs, de, es, fr, and hu because it improved the results on the dev set only for these languages.

simple-rule-based starts by linking each pronoun to the nearest previous noun of the same gender (as annotated in the provided CoNLL-U files) and then applies the "*berulasek*" post-processing.

The purpose of these two submissions was to show what results can be achieved with just a few lines of code and without using the training data.

Matouš Moravec submitted one system *moravec*. The system is based on postprocessing existing coreference prediction using named entity information. Specifically, the submission starts with baseline predictions, runs the NameTag web service[13] (Straková et al., 2019) on the underlying texts and applies the following three postprocessing rules using Udapi (Popel et al., 2017): (1) changing coreference spans to spans of named entities, (2) removing coreference links between different named entity types, and (3) adding coreference links between named entities of the same type that have a high string similarity. The author was not able to obtain any results that were better than the baseline for a whole dataset, although in some individual documents within these datasets coreference prediction was improved.

Karol Saputa submitted one system *k-sap* (for details see (Saputa, 2022) in this volume). It employs BERT-based antecedent scoring for possible spans based on representation of span start and end tokens. The submission employs the approach described by Kirstain et al. (2021).

5 Results and Comparison

The *straka* system by the ÚFAL CorPipe team is clearly the winner of the shared task. It surpasses other systems not only in terms of the primary score (see the *primary* column in Table 4) but consistently also in almost all coreference metrics, both in precision and recall (see Table 5).

Table 6 shows that systems submitted by the ÚFAL CorPipe team are dominant on the great majority of datasets. They are outperformed only by the *ondfa* system, namely on de_parcorfull and hu_szeged datasets. Per-dataset evaluation also reveals that the last place of the *k-sap* system in the overall ranking is unequivocally caused by ignoring all but the pl_pcc dataset where it ranks 3rd.

In comparison to the baseline system, most systems ouperformed it by a relatively large margin. The winning *straka* system achieves over 12 points in the primary score, which is more than 20% improvement over the baseline performance. This is an extremely beneficial effect of the shared task, which may drive further development in multilingual coreference resolution.

Results unsurprisingly also confirm a doubtless dominance of machine learning approaches. Although rule-based postprocessing has been employed by some teams (also encouraged by availability of the baseline predictions), its incorporation is either motivated by the nature of the primary score (*straka** systems) or it improves upon the baseline only marginally (the *berulasek* system) or not at all (the *moravec* system).

We observe almost the same picture in evaluation with singletons (see Table 4) – the *straka** systems outperforming all the other systems. Moreover, these submissions are the only ones that are positively affected by the inclusion of singletons. It suggests that unlike other teams, ÚFAL CorPipe have optimized for singletons as well (confirmed by statistics on mentions and entities in Table 9).

Interestingly, no system outperformed the baseline in the exact-match evaluation (see the *exact-match* column in Table 4). Considerably low scores compared to the partial matching setting are apparently caused by the choice of partial matching as part of the primary score, which most of the teams optimized for. Two teams (ÚFAL CorPipe and Barbora Dohnalová) even utilize the present dependency structure to reduce their mentions to heads only in post-processing (cf. Head matching in Section 3).[14] The preference of most systems in

[12]The *simple-rule-based* system was originally called *simple_baseline* in CodaLab, but we renamed it here to prevent confusing it with the official baseline (described in Section 4.1 and named *sidoj* in CodaLab).

[13]`http://lindat.mff.cuni.cz/services/nametag/api-reference.php`

[14]It would be interesting to evaluate the ÚFAL CorPipe (*straka**) systems before this post-processing, which slightly improves the primary metric (partial-match), but substantially worsens the exact-match.

underspecified mentions is confirmed by the head-match scores (Table 4), which are almost identical to the primary scores, and by MOR scores (see Table 5), reaching high precision but failing in recall.

5.1 Automatic analysis

To the best of our knowledge, this is the first shared task on multilingual coreference resolution that includes zeros. Therefore, Table 7 focuses more on the performance with respect to zero anaphora (cf. Table 1 for proportion of all zeros in the data). It shows anaphor-decomposable scores achieved by the systems on zeros across the datasets that comprise anaphoric zeros. The best-performing systems surpass 90 F1 points for most of the languages. Nevertheless, recall that the setup for zeros is slightly unrealistic as participants have been given the input documents with zeros (both anaphoric and non-anaphoric) already reconstructed.

We provide several additional tables in the appendices to shed more light on the differences between the submitted systems. Table 8 shows results factorized according the different part of speech tags in the mention heads. Tables 9–11 show various statistics on the entities and mentions in a concatenation of all the test sets. Tables 12–14 show the same statistics for cs_pcedt, which is the largest dataset in CorefUD 1.0.

5.2 Manual analysis

In addition to numerical scores, we also want to gain some insight into the types of errors that individual systems do. Such error analysis is inevitably incomplete, as we cannot manually check over 50,000 non-singleton mentions from all the test datasets, times eight system submissions. Nevertheless, here are some observations for illustration:

BASELINE, cs_pdt

It often does not recognize a mention. For example, adjectives derived from locations (*ostravské* "Ostrava-based") tend to be mentions in CorefUD, often nested ones (*ostravské firmy* "Ostrava-based companies") but the system does not recognize them. It also fails to recognize many mentions that are regular noun phrases.

Once the system detects a mention, it often has the correct mention span, although there are some odd failures, too.

In case of a newspaper interview, first and second person pronouns are recognized as mentions, coreference between mentions of the same person is found correctly, but their link to a person's name is easily misinterpreted.

straka, cs_pdt

It detects some mentions that BASELINE does not see (e.g. *ostravské*).

Linking names to first and second person pronouns is also a problem, although the system got right one instance where the baseline failed.

BASELINE, es_ancora

There is an even more dramatic disproportion between number of mentions found and those in the gold data. This is probably caused by the large number of singletons in AnCora.

On the other hand, it correctly identified mentions (including coreference) that were not annotated in the gold data: M_1 = *tanto China como Perú* "China as well as Peru", M_2 = *estas dos naciones* "these two nations".

Elsewhere, the coreference resolver got misled by similar titles of two different people: *el canciller peruano* "the Peruvian secretary" was linked to *el canciller chino* "the Chinese secretary".

straka, es_ancora

Much more successful in identifying mentions; unlike the baseline, it seems to be able to identify singletons.

Unlike the baseline, *straka* did not recognize *tanto China como Perú* as a mention. It also did not link the word *China* from this expression to a previous (singleton) instance of *China*; but since the same surprising annotation appears in the gold data, the system scored here.

6 Conclusions and Future Work

This paper summarizes the outcomes of the Multilingual Coreference Resolution Shared Task held with the CRAC 2022 workshop. We hope that the presented shared task establishes a new state of the art in multilingual coreference resolution.

Possible future editions of the shared task could be improved or extended along the following directions:

- We will fix minor errors in CorefUD's harmonization procedure that have been identified during the shared task.
- We would like to include additional datasets, especially for languages that have not been covered in CorefUD yet; about 20 resources

system	primary	head-match	exact-match	with-singletons
straka	**70.72**	**70.72** (+0.00)	33.18 (-37.54)	**72.98** (+2.26)
straka-single...	69.56	69.56 (+0.00)	33.06 (-36.51)	71.81 (+2.25)
ondfa	67.64	68.51 (+0.87)	54.73 (-12.91)	58.06 (-9.58)
straka-only...	64.30	64.30 (+0.00)	32.28 (-32.02)	67.93 (+3.63)
berulasek	59.72	59.72 (+0.00)	31.50 (-28.22)	50.84 (-8.88)
BASELINE	58.53	59.67 (+1.13)	**56.72** (-1.82)	49.69 (-8.84)
moravec	55.05	56.35 (+1.29)	52.68 (-2.37)	46.79 (-8.27)
simple-rule-based	18.14	18.14 (+0.00)	12.60 (-5.54)	17.13 (-1.00)
k-sap	5.90	5.93 (+0.03)	5.84 (-0.05)	3.83 (-2.07)

Table 4: Main results: the CoNLL metric macro-averaged over all datasets. The table shows the primary metric (partial-match, excluding singletons) and its three versions: head-match, exact-match and with-singletons. The best score in each column is in bold.

system	MUC	B^3	CEAF-e	BLANC	LEA	MOR
straka	**74** / 76 / **74**	**67 / 72 / 68**	**71 / 70 / 70**	**63** / 70 / **65**	**63 / 69 / 65**	32 / 83 / 45
straka-single...	72 / 76 / 73	65 / 72 / 67	67 / 70 / 68	61 / **71** / 64	62 / 68 / 64	32 / 84 / 45
ondfa	69 / **76** / 72	61 / 71 / 65	62 / 69 / 65	59 / 69 / 63	58 / 67 / 62	**52** / 84 / **62**
straka-only...	65 / 71 / 68	58 / 68 / 62	61 / 67 / 63	55 / 66 / 59	54 / 63 / 58	30 / 83 / 43
berulasek	58 / 76 / 64	50 / 70 / 57	52 / 67 / 58	46 / 70 / 53	45 / 66 / 53	27 / **88** / 40
BASELINE	56 / 74 / 63	48 / 69 / 56	51 / 66 / 57	45 / 68 / 51	44 / 64 / 51	49 / 86 / 61
moravec	53 / 70 / 60	45 / 65 / 52	50 / 59 / 53	41 / 59 / 46	41 / 60 / 48	49 / 81 / 60
simple-rule-based	14 / 22 / 16	14 / 26 / 17	23 / 27 / 22	10 / 20 / 11	7 / 17 / 9	16 / 55 / 23
k-sap	6 / 7 / 6	5 / 7 / 6	5 / 6 / 6	5 / 7 / 6	5 / 6 / 6	5 / 7 / 6

Table 5: Recall / Precision / F1 for individual secondary metrics. All scores macro-averaged over all datasets. Note that the high recall and F1 MOR scores of ONDFA (relative to STRAKA* systems) is caused by the fact that ONDFA does not use any post-processing restricting mention spans to the head.

system	ca_ancora	cs_pcedt	cs_pdt	de_parcorfull	de_potsdam	en_gum	en_parcorfull	es_ancora	fr_democrat	hu_szeged	lt_lcc	pl_pcc	ru_rucor
straka	78.18	**78.59**	**77.69**	65.52	70.69	72.50	**39.00**	**81.39**	**65.27**	63.15	**69.92**	78.12	**79.34**
straka-single...	**78.49**	78.49	77.57	59.94	**71.11**	**73.20**	33.55	80.80	64.35	63.38	67.38	**78.32**	77.74
ondfa	70.55	74.07	72.42	**73.90**	68.68	68.31	31.90	72.32	61.39	**65.01**	68.05	75.20	77.50
straka-only...	76.34	77.87	76.76	36.50	56.65	70.66	23.48	78.78	64.94	62.94	61.32	73.36	76.26
berulasek	64.67	70.56	67.95	38.50	57.70	63.07	36.44	66.61	56.04	55.02	65.67	65.99	68.17
BASELINE	63.74	70.00	67.27	33.75	55.44	62.59	36.44	65.99	55.55	52.35	64.81	65.34	67.66
moravec	58.25	68.19	64.71	31.86	52.84	59.15	36.44	62.01	54.87	52.00	59.49	63.40	52.49
simple-rule-based	15.58	5.51	9.48	29.81	19.41	21.99	11.37	16.64	21.74	17.00	27.53	15.69	24.06
k-sap	0.00	0.00	0.00	0.00	0.00	0.00	0.00	0.00	0.00	0.00	0.00	76.67	0.00

Table 6: Results for individual languages in the primary metric (CoNLL).

system	ca_ancora	cs_pdt	cs_pcedt	es_ancora	hu_szeged	pl_pcc
straka	**91** / 91 / **91**	**91** / **92** / **92**	87 / **90** / **89**	**94** / **95** / **95**	79 / 71 / 75	62 / 60 / 61
straka-single...	91 / **92** / 91	91 / 92 / 92	**88** / 90 / 89	94 / 95 / 95	76 / **76** / 76	**79** / 83 / **81**
ondfa	88 / 88 / 88	88 / 92 / 90	85 / 89 / 87	92 / 94 / 93	**81** / 74 / **77**	62 / 60 / 61
straka-only...	89 / 88 / 88	90 / 92 / 91	87 / 89 / 88	92 / 92 / 92	74 / 70 / 72	71 / 63 / 67
berulasek	82 / 83 / 82	84 / 86 / 85	80 / 84 / 82	87 / 89 / 88	55 / 54 / 54	42 / 50 / 45
BASELINE	82 / 82 / 82	84 / 86 / 85	80 / 83 / 82	87 / 88 / 87	52 / 51 / 52	42 / 50 / 45
moravec	81 / 82 / 82	84 / 85 / 84	80 / 83 / 81	87 / 88 / 87	52 / 51 / 52	42 / 50 / 45
simple-rule-based	0 / 0 / 0	0 / 0 / 0	0 / 0 / 0	0 / 0 / 0	0 / 0 / 0	0 / 0 / 0
k-sap	0 / 0 / 0	0 / 0 / 0	0 / 0 / 0	0 / 0 / 0	0 / 0 / 0	4 / **100** / 8

Table 7: Recall / Precision / F1 for anaphor-decomposable score of coreference resolution on zero anaphors across individual languages. Only the datasets that contain anaphoric zeros are listed (en_gum excluded as all zeros in its test set are non-anaphoric). Note that these scores are directly comparable neither to the CoNLL score nor to the supplementary scores calculated with respect to whole entities in Table 5.

that have not been harmonized yet due to various reasons are listed in Nedoluzhko et al. (2021a) (or have been harmonized, but cannot be distributed publicly because of license limitations).

- We will try to find ways to include also coreference data from the OntoNotes project, which would be extremely valuable because of their size, quality, and popularity.
- We will make the setup more realistic. Firstly, we will delete empty nodes from the test data to be processed by participants' systems. It also requires adjusting the scorer so that it can evaluate pairs of documents with different sets of empty nodes. Secondly, we will replace the manual morpho-syntax annotation with the automatic one for the shared task.
- We will consider introducing subtasks focused on other anaphoric relations than just identity coreference (see Yu et al. (2022) for a description of Universal Anaphora Scorer that is capable of evaluating also non-identity coreference relations); for instance, some CorefUD datasets contain hand-annotated bridging relations already now.

Acknowledgements

This work was supported by the Grant 20-16819X (LUSyD) of the Czech Science Foundation (GAČR); LM2018101 (LINDAT/CLARIAH-CZ) of the Ministry of Education, Youth, and Sports of the Czech Republic; FW03010656 of the Technology Agency of the Czech Republic; the European Regional Development Fund as a part of 2014–2020 Smart Growth Operational Programme, CLARIN — Common Language Resources and Technology Infrastructure, project no. POIR.04.02.00-00C002/19; the project co-financed by the Polish Ministry of Education and Science under the agreement 2022/WK/09; and SGS-2022-016 Advanced methods of data processing and analysis. We thank all the participants of the shared task for participating and for providing brief descriptions of their systems. We also thank two anonymous reviewers and Jana Straková for very insightful and useful remarks.

References

Amit Bagga and Breck Baldwin. 1998. Algorithms for scoring coreference chains. In *Proceedings of The First International Conference on Language Resources and Evaluation Workshop on Linguistics Coreference*, pages 563–566.

Peter Bourgonje and Manfred Stede. 2020. The Potsdam commentary corpus 2.2: Extending annotations for shallow discourse parsing. In *Proceedings of the 12th Language Resources and Evaluation Conference*, pages 1061–1066, Marseille, France. European Language Resources Association.

Sabine Buchholz and Erwin Marsi. 2006. CoNLL-X Shared Task on Multilingual Dependency Parsing.

In *Proceedings of the Tenth Conference on Computational Natural Language Learning (CoNLL-X)*, pages 149–164.

Hyung Won Chung, Thibault Févry, Henry Tsai, Melvin Johnson, and Sebastian Ruder. 2020. Rethinking embedding coupling in pre-trained language models. *CoRR*, abs/2010.12821.

Alexis Conneau, Kartikay Khandelwal, Naman Goyal, Vishrav Chaudhary, Guillaume Wenzek, Francisco Guzmán, Edouard Grave, Myle Ott, Luke Zettlemoyer, and Veselin Stoyanov. 2019. Unsupervised cross-lingual representation learning at scale. *CoRR*, abs/1911.02116.

Marie-Catherine de Marneffe, Christopher Manning, Joakim Nivre, and Daniel Zeman. 2021. Universal Dependencies. *Computational Linguistics*, 47(2):255–308.

Pascal Denis and Jason Baldridge. 2009. Global joint models for coreference resolution and named entity classification. *Proces. del Leng. Natural.*

Jacob Devlin, Ming-Wei Chang, Kenton Lee, and Kristina Toutanova. 2018. BERT: pre-training of deep bidirectional transformers for language understanding. *CoRR*, abs/1810.04805.

Jan Hajič, Eduard Bejček, Jaroslava Hlaváčová, Marie Mikulová, Milan Straka, Jan Štěpánek, and Barbora Štěpánková. 2020. Prague Dependency Treebank - Consolidated 1.0. In *Proceedings of the 12th International Conference on Language Resources and Evaluation (LREC 2020)*, pages 5208–5218, Marseille, France. European Language Resources Association.

Yuval Kirstain, Ori Ram, and Omer Levy. 2021. Coreference resolution without span representations. In *Proceedings of the 59th Annual Meeting of the Association for Computational Linguistics and the 11th International Joint Conference on Natural Language Processing (Volume 2: Short Papers)*, pages 14–19, Online. Association for Computational Linguistics.

Frédéric Landragin. 2021. Le corpus Democrat et son exploitation. Présentation. *Langages*, 224:11–24.

Ekaterina Lapshinova-Koltunski, Christian Hardmeier, and Pauline Krielke. 2018. ParCorFull: a Parallel Corpus Annotated with Full Coreference. In *Proceedings of the Eleventh International Conference on Language Resources and Evaluation (LREC 2018)*, Miyazaki, Japan. European Language Resources Association (ELRA).

Anke Lüdeling, Julia Ritz, Manfred Stede, and Amir Zeldes. 2016. Corpus Linguistics and Information Structure Research. In Caroline Féry and Shinichiro Ichihara, editors, *The Oxford Handbook of Information Structure*, pages 599–617. Oxford University Press.

Xiaoqiang Luo. 2005. On coreference resolution performance metrics. In *Proceedings of the Conference on Human Language Technology and Empirical Methods in Natural Language Processing*, HLT '05, pages 25–32. Association for Computational Linguistics.

Nafise Sadat Moosavi and Michael Strube. 2016. Which coreference evaluation metric do you trust? a proposal for a link-based entity aware metric. In *Proceedings of the 54th Annual Meeting of the Association for Computational Linguistics (Volume 1: Long Papers)*, pages 632–642, Berlin, Germany. Association for Computational Linguistics.

Anna Nedoluzhko, Michal Novák, Silvie Cinková, Marie Mikulová, and Jiří Mírovský. 2016. Coreference in Prague Czech-English Dependency Treebank. In *Proceedings of the Tenth International Conference on Language Resources and Evaluation (LREC'16)*, pages 169–176, Portorož, Slovenia. European Language Resources Association (ELRA).

Anna Nedoluzhko, Michal Novák, Martin Popel, Zdeněk Žabokrtský, and Daniel Zeman. 2021a. Coreference meets Universal Dependencies – a pilot experiment on harmonizing coreference datasets for 11 languages. Technical Report 66, ÚFAL MFF UK, Praha, Czechia.

Anna Nedoluzhko, Michal Novák, Martin Popel, Zdeněk Žabokrtskỳ, Amir Zeldes, and Daniel Zeman. 2022. Corefud 1.0: Coreference meets universal dependencies. In *Proceedings of LREC.*

Anna Nedoluzhko, Michal Novák, Martin Popel, Zdeněk Žabokrtský, and Daniel Zeman. 2021b. Is one head enough? Mention heads in coreference annotations compared with UD-style heads. In *Proceedings of the Sixth International Conference on Dependency Linguistics (Depling, SyntaxFest 2021)*, pages 101–114, Stroudsburg, PA, USA. Association for Computational Linguistics.

Maciej Ogrodniczuk, Katarzyna Glowińska, Mateusz Kopeć, Agata Savary, and Magdalena Zawisławska. 2013. Polish coreference corpus. In *Human Language Technology. Challenges for Computer Science and Linguistics - 6th Language and Technology Conference, LTC 2013, Poznań, Poland, December 7-9, 2013. Revised Selected Papers*, volume 9561 of *Lecture Notes in Computer Science*, pages 215–226. Springer.

Maciej Ogrodniczuk, Katarzyna Głowińska, Mateusz Kopeć, Agata Savary, and Magdalena Zawisławska. 2015. *Coreference in Polish: Annotation, Resolution and Evaluation.* Walter De Gruyter.

Martin Popel, Zdeněk Žabokrtský, Anna Nedoluzhko, Michal Novák, and Daniel Zeman. 2021. Do UD trees match mention spans in coreference annotations? In *Findings of the Association for Computational Linguistics: EMNLP 2021*, pages 3570–3576, Punta Cana, Dominican Republic. Association for Computational Linguistics.

Martin Popel, Zdeněk Žabokrtský, and Martin Vojtek. 2017. Udapi: Universal API for Universal Dependencies. In *NoDaLiDa 2017 Workshop on Universal Dependencies*, pages 96–101, Göteborg, Sweden. Göteborgs universitet.

Sameer Pradhan, Xiaoqiang Luo, Marta Recasens, Eduard Hovy, Vincent Ng, and Michael Strube. 2014. Scoring coreference partitions of predicted mentions: A reference implementation. In *Proceedings of the 52nd Annual Meeting of the Association for Computational Linguistics (Volume 2: Short Papers)*, pages 30–35, Baltimore, Maryland. Association for Computational Linguistics.

Sameer Pradhan, Alessandro Moschitti, Nianwen Xue, Olga Uryupina, and Yuchen Zhang. 2012. CoNLL-2012 shared task: Modeling multilingual unrestricted coreference in OntoNotes. In *Joint Conference on EMNLP and CoNLL - Shared Task*, pages 1–40, Jeju Island, Korea. Association for Computational Linguistics.

Ondřej Pražák, Miloslav Konopík, and Jakub Sido. 2021. Multilingual coreference resolution with harmonized annotations. In *Proceedings of the International Conference on Recent Advances in Natural Language Processing (RANLP 2021)*, pages 1119–1123.

Ondřej Pražák and Miloslav Konopik. 2022. End-to-end Multilingual Coreference Resolution with Mention Head Prediction. In *Proceedings of the CRAC 2022 Shared Task on Multilingual Coreference Resolution*. Association for Computational Linguistics.

Adam Przepiórkowski, Rafał L. Górski, Barbara Lewandowska-Tomaszyk, and Marek Łaziński. 2008. Towards the National Corpus of Polish. In *Proceedings of the Sixth International Conference on Language Resources and Evaluation (LREC'08)*, Marrakech, Morocco. European Language Resources Association (ELRA).

Marta Recasens and Eduard H. Hovy. 2011. BLANC: Implementing the rand index for coreference evaluation. *Natural Language Engineering*, 17(4):485–510. Tex.bibsource= dblp computer science bibliography, https://dblp.org tex.biburl= https://dblp.org/rec/bib/journals/nle/RecasensH11.

Marta Recasens, Lluís Màrquez, Emili Sapena, M. Antònia Martí, Mariona Taulé, Véronique Hoste, Massimo Poesio, and Yannick Versley. 2010. SemEval-2010 task 1: Coreference resolution in multiple languages. In *Proceedings of the 5th International Workshop on Semantic Evaluation*, pages 1–8, Uppsala, Sweden. Association for Computational Linguistics.

Marta Recasens and M. Antònia Martí. 2010. AnCora-CO: Coreferentially Annotated Corpora for Spanish and Catalan. *Lang. Resour. Eval.*, 44(4):315–345.

Karol Saputa. 2022. Coreference Resolution for Polish and Beyond: Description of the Herferencer System for the CRAC 2022 Shared Task on Multilingual Coreference Resolution. In *Proceedings of the CRAC 2022 Shared Task on Multilingual Coreference Resolution*. Association for Computational Linguistics.

Milan Straka. 2018. UDPipe 2.0 prototype at CoNLL 2018 UD shared task. In *Proceedings of the CoNLL 2018 Shared Task: Multilingual Parsing from Raw Text to Universal Dependencies*, pages 197–207, Brussels, Belgium. Association for Computational Linguistics.

Milan Straka and Jana Straková. 2022. ÚFAL CorPipe at CRAC 2022: Effectivity of Multilingual Models for Coreference Resolution. In *Proceedings of the CRAC 2022 Shared Task on Multilingual Coreference Resolution*. Association for Computational Linguistics.

Jana Straková, Milan Straka, and Jan Hajic. 2019. Neural architectures for nested NER through linearization. In *Proceedings of the 57th Annual Meeting of the Association for Computational Linguistics*, pages 5326–5331, Florence, Italy. Association for Computational Linguistics.

Mariona Taulé, M. Antònia Martí, and Marta Recasens. 2008. AnCora: Multilevel annotated corpora for Catalan and Spanish. In *Proceedings of the Sixth International Conference on Language Resources and Evaluation (LREC'08)*, Marrakech, Morocco. European Language Resources Association (ELRA).

Svetlana Toldova, Anna Roytberg, Alina Ladygina, Maria Vasilyeva, Ilya Azerkovich, Matvei Kurzukov, G. Sim, D.V. Gorshkov, A. Ivanova, Anna Nedoluzhko, and Yulia Grishina. 2014. Evaluating Anaphora and Coreference Resolution for Russian. In *Komp'juternaja lingvistika i intellektual'nye tehnologii. Po materialam ezhegodnoj Mezhdunarodnoj konferencii Dialog*, pages 681–695.

Don Tuggener. 2014. Coreference resolution evaluation for higher level applications. In *Proceedings of the 14th Conference of the European Chapter of the Association for Computational Linguistics, volume 2: Short Papers*, pages 231–235, Gothenburg, Sweden. Association for Computational Linguistics.

Olga Uryupina, Ron Artstein, Antonella Bristot, Federica Cavicchio, Francesca Delogu, Kepa J. Rodriguez, and Massimo Poesio. 2020. Annotating a broad range of anaphoric phenomena, in a variety of genres: the ARRAU Corpus. *Natural Language Engineering*, 26(1):95–128.

Marc Vilain, John Burger, John Aberdeen, Dennis Connolly, and Lynette Hirschman. 1995. A model-theoretic coreference scoring scheme. In *Sixth Message Understanding Conference (MUC-6): Proceedings of a Conference Held in Columbia, Maryland, November 6-8, 1995.*

Veronika Vincze, Klára Hegedűs, Alex Sliz-Nagy, and Richárd Farkas. 2018. SzegedKoref: A Hungarian coreference corpus. In *Proceedings of the Eleventh*

International Conference on Language Resources and Evaluation (LREC 2018), Miyazaki, Japan. European Language Resources Association (ELRA).

Rodrigo Wilkens, Bruno Oberle, Frédéric Landragin, and Amalia Todirascu. 2020. French coreference for spoken and written language. In *Proceedings of the 12th Language Resources and Evaluation Conference*, pages 80–89, Marseille, France. European Language Resources Association.

Juntao Yu, Sopan Khosla, Nafise Sadat Moosavi, Silviu Paun, Sameer Pradhan, and Massimo Poesio. 2022. The universal anaphora scorer. In *Proceedings of the Language Resources and Evaluation Conference*, pages 4873–4883, Marseille, France. European Language Resources Association.

Amir Zeldes. 2017. The GUM Corpus: Creating Multilayer Resources in the Classroom. *Language Resources and Evaluation*, 51(3):581–612.

Voldemaras Žitkus and Rita Butkienė. 2018. Coreference Annotation Scheme and Corpus for Lithuanian Language. In *Fifth International Conference on Social Networks Analysis, Management and Security, SNAMS 2018, Valencia, Spain, October 15-18, 2018*, pages 243–250. IEEE.

A Partial CoNLL results by head UPOS

system	NOUN	PRON	PROPN	DET	ADJ	VERB	ADV	NUM
straka	**68.71**	**73.72**	**72.29**	66.58	47.71	**38.44**	**49.85**	**48.30**
straka-single...	67.17	73.25	70.35	62.65	**49.84**	36.91	45.77	44.97
ondfa	66.04	71.43	70.72	**69.01**	39.67	25.47	38.51	33.52
straka-only...	61.46	67.08	63.89	60.60	41.38	30.71	35.70	39.55
berulasek	56.43	61.55	59.47	48.91	32.74	18.37	23.67	31.02
BASELINE	55.24	60.44	58.23	48.65	30.43	18.29	23.44	29.87
moravec	52.91	58.82	52.43	46.80	27.49	18.19	23.41	29.22
simple-rule-based	10.22	18.27	17.78	6.32	2.96	3.31	1.58	4.97
k-sap	5.74	5.80	5.99	5.84	4.72	5.77	4.08	5.98

Table 8: CoNLL F1 score evaluated only on entities with heads of a given UPOS. In both the gold and prediction files we deleted some entities before running the evaluation. We kept only entities with at least one mention with a given head UPOS (universal part of speech tag). For the purpose of this analysis, if the head node had deprel=flat children, their UPOS tags were considered as well, so for example in "Mr./NOUN Brown/PROPN" both NOUN and PROPN were taken as head UPOS, so the entity with this mention will be reported in both columns NOUN and PROPN. Otherwise, the CoNLL F1 scores are the same as in the primary metric, i.e. an unweighted average over all datasets, partial-match, without singletons. Note that when distinguishing entities into events and nominal entities, the VERB column can be considered as an approximation of the performance on events. One of the limitations of this approach is that copula is not treated as head in the Universal Dependencies, so e.g. phrase *She is nice* is not considered for the VERB column, but for the ADJ column (head of the phrase is *nice*).

B Statistics of the submitted systems on concatenation of all test sets

	entities				distribution of lengths				
system	total	per 1k	length		1	2	3	4	5+
	count	words	max	avg.	[%]	[%]	[%]	[%]	[%]
gold	41,001	104	509	2.2	54.9	23.5	9.2	4.3	8.0
BASELINE	4,541	11	217	11.2	0.0	33.1	8.6	6.0	52.3
berulasek	4,583	12	242	11.1	0.4	32.8	8.9	6.1	51.8
k-sap	1,744	4	41	4.0	0.1	50.1	18.8	8.6	22.4
moravec	5,469	14	210	10.8	1.8	28.2	9.6	4.6	55.8
ondfa	4,628	12	174	11.7	0.0	31.6	9.5	5.4	53.5
simple-rule-based	1,729	4	149	16.3	0.0	4.5	1.3	7.8	86.5
straka	12,669	32	200	7.1	27.1	4.5	3.6	6.8	58.0
straka-only...	12,552	32	338	7.2	25.5	4.4	4.1	7.3	58.7
straka-single...	12,669	32	243	7.1	26.2	4.4	4.0	6.9	58.5

Table 9: Statistics on coreference entities. The total number of entities and the average number of entities per 1000 tokens in the running text. The maximum and average entity "length", i.e., number of mentions in the entity. Distribution of entity lengths (singletons have length = 1).

system	mentions				distribution of lengths					
	total	per 1k	length		0	1	2	3	4	5+
	count	words	max	avg.	[%]	[%]	[%]	[%]	[%]	[%]
gold	69,406	175	104	3.3	10.2	39.4	19.6	8.5	4.4	17.9
BASELINE	50,783	128	26	2.2	13.3	46.3	19.1	7.3	3.4	10.7
berulasek	50,935	129	1	0.9	13.4	86.6	0.0	0.0	0.0	0.0
k-sap	6,941	18	29	1.6	0.0	75.1	14.1	4.1	2.0	4.7
moravec	58,883	149	26	2.1	11.5	50.2	18.5	7.2	3.2	9.5
ondfa	54,018	137	30	1.7	12.5	65.8	9.6	3.8	1.9	6.4
simple-rule-based	28,130	71	1	1.0	0.0	100.0	0.0	0.0	0.0	0.0
straka	86,412	218	1	0.9	8.4	91.6	0.0	0.0	0.0	0.0
straka-only...	87,059	220	1	0.9	8.4	91.6	0.0	0.0	0.0	0.0
straka-single...	86,689	219	1	0.9	8.4	91.6	0.0	0.0	0.0	0.0

Table 10: Statistics on non-singleton mentions. The total number of mentions and the average number of mentions per 1000 words of running text. The maximum and average mention length, i.e., number of nonempty nodes in the mention. Distribution of mention lengths (zeros have length = 0).

system	mention type [%]			distribution of head UPOS [%]								
	w/empty	w/gap	non-tree	NOUN	PRON	PROPN	DET	ADJ	VERB	ADV	NUM	other
gold	9.9	0.7	2.6	52.6	17.9	13.9	5.4	2.5	3.5	1.0	1.1	2.0
BASELINE	15.0	0.0	2.1	38.7	28.6	14.0	8.4	2.6	3.9	1.1	0.3	2.3
berulasek	13.4	0.0	0.0	38.2	28.5	14.7	8.4	2.6	3.8	1.1	0.3	2.2
k-sap	0.2	0.0	1.5	39.9	14.1	13.3	3.0	1.2	19.5	0.5	0.1	8.4
moravec	12.9	0.0	2.4	35.0	24.6	21.7	7.7	2.3	3.5	1.0	0.4	3.9
ondfa	13.3	0.0	1.4	40.7	27.6	13.6	8.1	2.6	3.6	1.2	0.4	2.3
simple-rule-based	0.0	0.0	0.0	15.6	62.6	21.8	0.0	0.0	0.0	0.0	0.0	0.0
straka	8.1	0.0	0.0	52.4	18.4	13.9	5.6	2.2	3.5	0.9	1.1	2.1
straka-only...	8.1	0.0	0.0	52.0	18.3	14.0	5.5	2.3	3.8	0.9	1.0	2.2
straka-single...	8.1	0.0	0.0	52.4	18.3	14.1	5.6	2.2	3.5	0.8	1.0	2.1

Table 11: Detailed statistics on mentions. The left part of the table shows percentage of: mentions with at least one empty node (w/empty); mentions with at least one gap, i.e. discontinuous mentions (w/gap); and non-treelet mentions, i.e. mentions not forming a connected subgraph in the dependency tree (non-tree). Note that these three types of mentions may be overlapping. The right part of the table shows distribution of mentions based on the universal part-of-speech tag (UPOS) of the head word. Note that the participants were not required to predict the head, so we used Udapi block `corefud.MoveHead` on all submissions for the purpose of these statistics.

C Statistics of the submitted systems on cs_pcedt

system	entities				distribution of lengths				
	total	per 1k	length		1	2	3	4	5+
	count	words	max	avg.	[%]	[%]	[%]	[%]	[%]
gold	2,533	45	89	3.3	1.8	63.7	14.8	6.4	13.3
BASELINE	2,048	37	78	3.5	0.0	62.1	16.5	6.1	15.4
berulasek	2,062	37	80	3.5	0.7	62.2	15.8	6.0	15.3
moravec	2,284	41	77	3.6	2.1	55.8	18.3	6.8	16.9
ondfa	2,136	38	74	3.5	0.0	61.9	16.1	6.3	15.7
simple-rule-based	271	5	57	6.1	0.0	46.1	14.4	11.1	28.4
straka	2,770	49	81	3.0	16.4	50.1	15.2	6.4	11.9
straka-only...	2,741	49	80	3.0	16.9	48.9	15.0	6.8	12.4
straka-single...	2,773	49	82	3.0	18.1	48.6	15.3	6.1	11.9

Table 12: Statistics on coreference entities in cs_pcedt.

system	mentions				distribution of lengths					
	total	per 1k	length		0	1	2	3	4	5+
	count	words	max	avg.	[%]	[%]	[%]	[%]	[%]	[%]
gold	8,365	149	61	3.6	22.6	26.9	17.4	8.6	3.9	20.6
BASELINE	7,258	129	22	2.5	24.6	28.2	18.7	9.0	4.1	15.4
berulasek	7,262	130	1	0.8	24.9	75.1	0.0	0.0	0.0	0.0
moravec	8,228	147	22	2.4	21.7	31.7	19.2	9.2	4.1	14.1
ondfa	7,527	134	21	2.7	23.4	27.4	18.3	9.0	4.5	17.3
simple-rule-based	1,640	29	1	1.0	0.0	100.0	0.0	0.0	0.0	0.0
straka	7,890	141	1	0.8	24.0	76.0	0.0	0.0	0.0	0.0
straka-only...	7,888	141	1	0.8	24.1	75.9	0.0	0.0	0.0	0.0
straka-single...	7,831	140	1	0.8	24.1	75.9	0.0	0.0	0.0	0.0

Table 13: Statistics on non-singleton mentions in cs_pcedt.

system	mention type [%]			distribution of head UPOS [%]								
	w/empty	w/gap	non-tree	NOUN	PRON	PROPN	DET	ADJ	VERB	ADV	NUM	other
gold	29.2	1.2	4.5	44.9	28.0	6.4	12.4	0.9	2.7	1.5	0.7	2.6
BASELINE	28.3	0.0	3.8	45.1	30.2	6.4	12.2	0.6	1.5	1.3	0.7	2.0
berulasek	24.9	0.0	0.0	44.6	30.1	7.2	12.2	0.5	1.5	1.3	0.7	1.9
moravec	24.8	0.0	3.8	41.5	26.5	12.4	10.7	0.6	1.3	1.1	0.7	5.2
ondfa	27.5	0.0	3.5	45.3	29.0	6.1	12.7	0.7	2.0	1.4	0.6	2.3
simple-rule-based	0.0	0.0	0.0	3.4	78.2	18.4	0.0	0.0	0.0	0.0	0.0	0.0
straka	23.3	0.0	0.0	45.0	28.1	5.9	12.7	0.8	2.7	1.3	0.7	2.8
straka-only...	23.2	0.0	0.0	44.9	28.2	6.1	12.5	1.0	2.8	1.3	0.6	2.7
straka-single...	23.3	0.0	0.0	45.0	28.2	6.0	12.7	0.8	2.6	1.3	0.6	2.8

Table 14: Detailed statistics on mentions in cs_pcedt.

Coreference Resolution for Polish: Improvements within the CRAC 2022 Shared Task

Karol Saputa
Institute of Computer Science, Polish Academy of Sciences, Warsaw, Poland
karol.saputa@ipipan.waw.pl

Abstract

The paper presents our system for coreference resolution in Polish. We compare the system with previous works for the Polish language as well as with the multilingual approach in the CRAC 2022 Shared Task on Multilingual Coreference Resolution thanks to a universal, multilingual data format and evaluation tool. We discuss the accuracy, computational performance, and evaluation approach of the new System which is a faster, end-to-end solution.

1 Introduction

The paper describes our approach to coreference resolution in the Polish language submitted to the CRAC 2022 Shared Task on Multilingual Coreference Resolution.

The scope of the Shared Task was multilingual systems for 10 languages included in CorefUD 1.0 (Nedoluzhko et al., 2022). However, here we focus mainly on the improvements for the Polish language within this task and present end-to-end coreference resolution for Polish.

2 Related Work

There are two important types of references for our work: the evaluation methods for coreference resolution and previous solutions for the Polish language.

2.1 Evaluation

The popular standard for coreference resolution was created during CoNLL-2011 Shared Task as an average of MUC, B-cubed, and CEAFe scores. It is also used in the CRAC 2022 Shared Task on Multilingual Coreference Resolution.

Previous implementations included Perl script evaluation of annotation in CoNNL-U (Pradhan et al., 2014). Similarly, there is a Scoreference[1] tool Java implementation including additionally CEAFm, and BLANC, which operates on TEI (Consortium, 2022) or MMAX2 (Müller and Strube, 2006) files. It was used in the evaluation of most coreference resolution tools for the Polish language because of its compatibility with Polish Coreference Corpus (Ogrodniczuk et al., 2016) data formats.

CorefUD dataset integrates Polish Coreference Corpus and many others into one format compatible with Universal Dependencies datasets and presents a new Python reimplementation of the metric CorefUD scorer[2]. Thanks to that, there is a clear way to evaluate and compare different coreference systems.

2.2 Coreference Resolution in Polish

The current state-of-the-art solution was a Corneferencer system (Nitoń et al., 2018). It is a system based only on mention clustering i.e. it requires a text with already correctly detected mentions which are further grouped into coreference clusters and remaining singleton mentions.

The mention pairs need to have labeled heads e.g. from a dependency parsing due to input features including embedding representation of mention head token. There are other hand-crafted features e.g. mention type, mention pair distance, and mention tokens' lemmas.

It also requires the generation of mention-pairs representations which in the highest scoring version (`all2all`) results in $O(n^2)$ complexity for all mention pairs passed to the system.

The Corneferencer system achieved 81.23 F1 CoNLL (Pradhan et al., 2011) measure in the best setting during evaluation on gold mentions.

3 System description

3.1 Architecture

The submitted system is based on the `start-to-end` system (Kirstain et al.).

[1] http://zil.ipipan.waw.pl/Scoreference

[2] https://github.com/ufal/corefud-scorer

Proceedings of the CRAC 2022 Shared Task on Multilingual Coreference Resolution, pages 18–22
October 17, 2022

This system was developed for English and is based on transformer architecture for natural language processing. It extends the Shared Task baseline system (Pražák et al., 2021) with the simplified mention-candidate representation.

3.1.1 Input features

Pre-trained model The words representation is based on the HerBERT[3] (Mroczkowski et al., 2021) pre-trained, BERT-based text encoder for the Polish language. The model has a maximum input length of 512 tokens so the longer texts are passed split (on sentence ends when possible).

End-to-end features The system works in an end-to-end fashion (Lee et al., 2017) with text-only input. In its original version (Kirstain et al.) based on the OntoNotes dataset (Weischedel et al., 2013), it included some additional annotations such as genre and speaker information which was not used here.

Such annotation is not available for the Polish dataset. Furthermore, hand-crafted features like speaker information hamper production deployment of the System.

3.1.2 Mentions

Mention representation Mention candidates are all spans of tokens (up to maximum length). Representations of candidates are based on the representation of the start and end tokens. Span representation is made to represent features related to the span is a mention.

Mention scoring Mentions are scored by calculating the biaffine combination of start and end token representations. Scores are used to prune the least scored spans from the mention candidates list.

3.1.3 Antecedents

Antecedent representation Antecedent representations are produced similarly to the mention representation except using a separate set of weights. Antecedent representation is made to represent coreference features.

Antecedent scoring Antecedents are scored by calculating the biaffine combination of two spans as concatenated start and end representations. The antecedent score measures whether two mentions are coreferent.

[3] `allegro/herbert-large-cased`

3.2 Linguistic modeling constraints

The biggest advantage of the architecture is its simplicity and low computational complexity. There are several constraints imposed by this architecture for application to Polish Coreference Corpus annotations.

3.2.1 Nested mentions

It is important for the architecture to recognize nested spans and match them with different entities. For example "the Association of Youth filmmakers" consists of two nested mentions coreferent with the association and the filmmakers. So it is needed to handle overlapping, nested spans. It is possible in `start-to-end` architecture by including all possible spans.

3.2.2 Singleton and mention head recognition

Polish Coreference Corpus includes annotation of singletons - mentions that have no coreferent mentions.

Scoring during the CRAC 2022 Shared Task on Multilingual Coreference Resolution omits singletons. `Start-to-end` architecture does not detect singletons as the spans are scored for the antecedent relation in pairs and it is the only element of the loss function (and model optimization). Singletons may not be included in the detected mentions since they should not be considered in antecedent scoring.

Including singletons in the task would need a modification of the loss function or adding an additional model.

3.3 Data augmentation

Polish Coreference Corpus consists of about 1800 documents consisting of one or more paragraphs of text, each originating from one source. Samples used for training included the original texts and subsamples.

Paragraphs and pairs of sentences were treated as additional separate subsamples that can be added to training samples. The coreference annotation was filtered to include only relations inside the sample.

The process of augmentation was controlled by parameters of a fraction of sentence pairs and paragraphs to include in the training sample.

Using samples of shorter lengths was important to improve performance on short texts.

3.4 Training

Dynamic batching There was dynamic batching

System	Precision	Recall	F1
submission	88.11	71.22	78.77
herbert–base	86.83	75.33	80.67
herbert–large	86.26	80.60	83.33

Table 1: Mention detection F1 measure results for Polish on the development set, singletons excluded.

System	F1
submission	63.64
herbert–base	72.44
herbert–large	73.39
corneferencer	82.44

Table 2: CoNLL F1 measure results for coreference resolution in Polish on the development set, singletons excluded.

applied - a constant maximum total batch length of texts. It was important in batching samples of different sizes e.g. short and long texts, and sentence pairs.

Optimization Model was optimized using PyTorch `AdamW` implementation with learning rate (1e-5), linear decay, and warm-up steps (5000) as recommended in `start-to-end` implementation[4].

4 Results

We compare metrics speed for the System with the Corneferencer and other submissions.

4.1 Performance

4.1.1 Mention detection

Mention detection is an important element of the system. Lack of detected spans impacts coreference resolution measures. Results are presented in Table 1.

Redundant spans do not lower performance because they can be assigned no coreference relation (null span antecedent). It corresponds to the higher precision of the system. Improving mention detection could be the first element of the overall improvement.

4.1.2 Coreference Resolution

Corneferencer comparison The previous solution for Polish, Corneferencer, was tested on gold mention annotation because the mentions are needed to process texts with this tool and used available model[5] , thus a different subset of PCC was used for comparison in Table 2, 200 texts from the test split used in Corneferencer evaluation.

Pre-trained models We compared the base (12 layers, `herbert-base`) and large (24 layers, `herbert-large`) version of the pre-trained encoder used in the System. The results are presented in Table 2. The smaller model was trained 71 000 steps and the larger one with 45 000 steps. The larger model gave a 1.31% improvement, with a 1.7% increase gained in the last 10 000 steps (F1 difference between 35 000 training steps and the final one). One step is one optimization step of the model.

Training step	Train F1	Dev F1	Difference
1000	1.56	0.87	0.69
5000	26.46	24.72	1.74
10000	58.73	55.45	3.28
15000	77.65	66.10	11.55
20000	84.81	69.31	15.50
25000	89.96	71.40	18.56
30000	92.90	72.10	20.81
35000	95.01	72.24	22.77
40000	96.03	72.63	23.40
45000	96.88	73.46	23.43

Table 3: Comparison of the development set generalization of the System during training, F1 evaluation of training and development sets.

4.2 Development set generalization

Comparison of the development set generalization of the System during training is presented in Table 3. As presented in (Yang et al.), it is a behavior of the big models, such as BERT-based models, to overcome the bias-variance tradeoff. The increasing difference between training and development sets does not impact model generalization.

4.3 Multilingual generalization

The System was tested on other languages in the Shared Task to test the degree of performance drop in such a zero-shot setting. Results are presented in Table 4. There was no attempt to use a multilingual pre-trained model or training on the other languages. The best result, 41.84, was achieved on the English dataset, the architecture used in the System was initially used for this language.

[4]`https://github.com/yuvalkirstain/s2e-coref`

[5]`http://zil.ipipan.waw.pl/Corneferencer?action=AttachFile&do=view&target=model_1190_features.h5`

Dataset	F1
en_parcorfull	22.34
de_parcorfull	13.67
lt_lcc	21.91
en_gum	41.84
es_ancora	21.87
fr_democrat	0.0
cs_pcedt	23.67
cs_pdt	27.94
ru_rucor	17.88
ca_ancora	17.49
pl_pcc	76.67
de_potsdamcc	40.59
hu_szegedkoref	11.45
average	25.95

Table 4: CoNLL F1 measure results for the System for all languages - trained only on Polish corpus with pre-trained model for Polish. Value for fr_democrat was not calculated due to technical issues.

System	Time [s]
herbert–large (GPU)	0.0542
herbert–large (CPU)	0.1845
corneferencer	271.7

Table 5: Document processing time - comparison of processing speed between `start-to-end` architecture and Corneferencer - previous solution for Polish. The

4.4 Processing speed

For the comparison of the System with the previous solution for Polish an important aspect is also the processing speed. Table 5 presents the results of comparison for Corneferencer and GPU/CPU versions of the System. Corneferencer time was calculated as a mean of two executions for three randomly chosen texts, and the System time was calculated as a mean over the test set.

Time included in the Corneferencer processing does not include e.g. mention detection. It is not a total time needed for the coreference resolution task and still, it is three orders of magnitude longer.

4.5 Submission

The model submitted to the Shared Task achieved a score of 76.67 F1 measure on the Polish test set. The submission was named `k-sap`. It was not the best result for Polish in the competition. It was overtaken by `straka` (78.12 F1, 1.019% improvement) and `straka-single-multilingual-model` (78.32 F1, 1.022%) which were multilingual submissions.

Submission	F1 Polish
straka-single-multilingual-model	78.32
straka	78.12
k-sap	76.67
ondfa	75.20
straka-only-single-treebank-data	73.36

Table 6: CRAC 2022 Shared Task on Multilingual Coreference Resolution Evaluation results for Polish, top 5 results.

The submitted model was undertrained (Section 4.2), and the train-dev difference was 9.77 F1 points. The results of the submission model on the Corneferencer dataset are lower (Table 2). There could have been test data leakage from original TEI files which we did not think was possible during the submission phase.

5 Further Work

Longformer There is a Longformer model for Polish available on Hugging Face Models[6]. It could improve results for longer texts (which are included in the Polish test set). However, it is not popular yet and was not tested.

Multilingual comparison 4 Shared Task submissions achieved above 60 F1 score, all of which gained more than 70 F1 for the Polish test subset. A comparison of these methods should help to answer questions: (1) is there still a need for a language-specific solution, (2) whether there are issues with data quality between corpora for different languages that could be improved by using guidelines from top-scored datasets.

6 Summary

For Polish, the System is faster, end-to-end, and has comparable performance to the previous solution.

There is a need to analyze other submissions to assess the state of language-specific systems' performance, however, we see that there is a capability to build a high-performing multilingual system.

The presence of a multilingual dataset and evaluation tool provides the infrastructure to build such a system efficiently and track progress.

[6] `sdadas/polish-longformer-large-4096`

Acknowledgements

This work was supported by the European Regional Development Fund as a part of 2014–2020 Smart Growth Operational Programme, CLARIN — Common Language Resources and Technology Infrastructure, project no. POIR.04.02.00-00C002/19 and by the project co-financed by the Minister of Education and Science under the agreement 2022/WK/09.

References

TEI Consortium. 2022. TEI P5: Guidelines for Electronic Text Encoding and Interchange. Publisher: Zenodo Version Number: v4.4.0.

Yuval Kirstain, Ori Ram, and Omer Levy. Coreference resolution without span representations. In *Proceedings of the 59th Annual Meeting of the Association for Computational Linguistics and the 11th International Joint Conference on Natural Language Processing (Volume 2: Short Papers)*, pages 14–19. Association for Computational Linguistics.

Kenton Lee, Luheng He, Mike Lewis, and Luke Zettlemoyer. 2017. End-to-end neural coreference resolution. In *Proceedings of the 2017 Conference on Empirical Methods in Natural Language Processing*, pages 188–197, Copenhagen, Denmark. Association for Computational Linguistics.

Robert Mroczkowski, Piotr Rybak, Alina Wróblewska, and Ireneusz Gawlik. 2021. HerBERT: Efficiently pretrained transformer-based language model for Polish. In *Proceedings of the 8th Workshop on Balto-Slavic Natural Language Processing*, pages 1–10, Kiyv, Ukraine. Association for Computational Linguistics.

Christoph Müller and Michael Strube. 2006. Multilevel annotation of linguistic data with MMAX2. In Sabine Braun, Kurt Kohn, and Joybrato Mukherjee, editors, *Corpus Technology and Language Pedagogy: New Resources, New Tools, New Methods*, pages 197–214. Peter Lang, Frankfurt a.M., Germany.

Anna Nedoluzhko, Michal Novák, Martin Popel, Zdeněk Žabokrtský, Amir Zeldes, Daniel Zeman, Peter Bourgonje, Silvie Cinková, Jan Hajič, Christian Hardmeier, Pauline Krielke, Frédéric Landragin, Ekaterina Lapshinova-Koltunski, M. Antònia Martí, Marie Mikulová, Maciej Ogrodniczuk, Marta Recasens, Manfred Stede, Milan Straka, Svetlana Toldova, Veronika Vincze, and Voldemaras Žitkus. 2022. Coreference in universal dependencies 1.0 (CorefUD 1.0). LINDAT/CLARIAH-CZ digital library at the Institute of Formal and Applied Linguistics (ÚFAL), Faculty of Mathematics and Physics, Charles University.

Bartłomiej Nitoń, Paweł Morawiecki, and Maciej Ogrodniczuk. 2018. Deep neural networks for coreference resolution for Polish. In *Proceedings of the Eleventh International Conference on Language Resources and Evaluation (LREC 2018)*, Miyazaki, Japan. European Language Resources Association (ELRA).

Maciej Ogrodniczuk, Katarzyna Głowińska, Mateusz Kopeć, Agata Savary, and Magdalena Zawisławska. 2016. Polish Coreference Corpus. In *Human Language Technology. Challenges for Computer Science and Linguistics*, Lecture Notes in Computer Science, pages 215–226, Cham. Springer International Publishing.

Sameer Pradhan, Xiaoqiang Luo, Marta Recasens, Eduard Hovy, Vincent Ng, and Michael Strube. 2014. Scoring coreference partitions of predicted mentions: A reference implementation. In *Proceedings of the 52nd Annual Meeting of the Association for Computational Linguistics (Volume 2: Short Papers)*, pages 30–35, Baltimore, Maryland. Association for Computational Linguistics.

Sameer Pradhan, Lance Ramshaw, Mitchell Marcus, Martha Palmer, Ralph Weischedel, and Nianwen Xue. 2011. CoNLL-2011 Shared Task: Modeling Unrestricted Coreference in OntoNotes. In *Proceedings of the Fifteenth Conference on Computational Natural Language Learning: Shared Task*, pages 1–27, Portland, Oregon, USA. Association for Computational Linguistics.

Ondřej Pražák, Miloslav Konopík, and Jakub Sido. 2021. Multilingual coreference resolution with harmonized annotations. In *Proceedings of the International Conference on Recent Advances in Natural Language Processing (RANLP 2021)*, pages 1119–1123, Held Online. INCOMA Ltd.

Ralph Weischedel, Martha Palmer, Mitchell Marcus, Eduard Hovy, Sameer Pradhan, Lance Ramshaw, Nianwen Xue, Ann Taylor, Jeff Kaufman, Michelle Franchini, Mohammed El-Bachouti, Robert Belvin, and Ann Houston. 2013. OntoNotes Release 5.0. Artwork Size: 2806280 KB Pages: 2806280 KB Type: dataset.

Zitong Yang, Yaodong Yu, Chong You, Jacob Steinhardt, and Yi Ma. Rethinking bias-variance trade-off for generalization of neural networks. In *Proceedings of the 37th International Conference on Machine Learning*, pages 10767–10777. PMLR. ISSN: 2640-3498.

End-to-end Multilingual Coreference Resolution with Mention Head Prediction

Ondřej Pražák and **Miloslav Konopík**

{ondfa,konopik}@kiv.zcu.cz

Department of Computer Science and Engineering,
NTIS – New Technologies for the Information Society,
Faculty of Applied Sciences, University of West Bohemia, Technická 8, 306 14 Plzeň
Czech Republic

Abstract

This paper describes our approach to the CRAC 2022 Shared Task on Multilingual Coreference Resolution. Our model is based on a state-of-the-art end-to-end coreference resolution system. Apart from joined multilingual training, we improved our results with mention head prediction. We also tried to integrate dependency information into our model. Our system ended up in 3rd place. Moreover, we reached the best performance on two datasets out of 13.

1 Introduction

Coreference resolution is the task of finding language expressions that refer to the same real-world entity (antecedent) of a given text. Sometimes the corefering expressions can come from a single sentence. However, the expressions can be one or more sentences apart as well. It is necessary to see the whole document in some hard cases to judge whether two expressions are corefering adequately. This task can be divided into two subtasks. Identifying entity mentions, and grouping the mentions together according to the real-world entity they refer to. The task of coreference resolution is closely related to anaphora resolution – see (Sukthanker et al., 2020) to compare these two tasks.

This paper describes our approach to the CRAC 2022 Shared Task on Multilingual Coreference Resolution. The task is based on the CorefUD dataset (Nedoluzhko et al., 2022). The CorefUD corpus contains 13 different datasets for ten languages in a harmonized scheme. As the CorefUD is meant to be the extension of Universal Dependencies with coreference annotation, all the datasets in CorefUD are treebanks. For some languages, human annotators provided the dependency annotations. For others, the annotation is created automatically with a parser. The coreference annotation is built upon the dependencies. This means that the mentions are subtrees in the dependency tree and can be represented with the head. In fact, in some of the datasets, there are non-treelet mentions – the mentions which do not form a single subtree. But even for these non-treelet mentions, a single headword is selected. There are some notable differences between the datasets. One of the most prominent ones is the presence of singletons. Singletons are clusters that contain only one mention. Singletons are not present in any coreference relation. However, they are annotated as mentions. For details about the dataset, please see Nedoluzhko et al. (2022) or Nedoluzhko et al. (2021). The task was simplified to predict only non-singleton mentions and group them into entity clusters.

For evaluation, the CorefUD scorer[1] is provided. The primary evaluation score is the CoNLL F_1 score with partial mention matching and singletons excluded. In the CorefUD scorer, a system mention matches a gold mention if all its words are included in the gold mention, and one of them is the key head. This means that the minimal correct span is the head, and it might be beneficial to predict mentions as only the heads.

2 Model

Our model builds on the official transformer-based end-to-end baseline (Pražák et al., 2021). The underlying neural end-to-end coreference resolution model was originally proposed by Lee et al. (2017). The model predicts the antecedents directly from all possible mention spans without a previous discrete decision about mentions. In the training phase, it maximizes the marginal log-likelihood of all correct antecedents:

$$J(D) = \log \prod_{i=1}^{N} \sum_{\hat{y} \in Y(i) \cap \text{GOLD}(i)} P(\hat{y}) \quad (1)$$

[1] https://github.com/ufal/corefud-scorer

Proceedings of the CRAC 2022 Shared Task on Multilingual Coreference Resolution, pages 23–27
October 17, 2022

CorefUD dataset	Total size					
	docs	sents	words	empty	singletons	discont.
Catalan-AnCora	1550	16,678	488,379	6,377	74.6%	0%
Czech-PDT	3165	49,428	834,721	33,086	35.3%	3.1%
Czech-PCEDT	2312	49,208	1,155,755	45,158	1.4%	4.1%
English-GUM	150	7,408	134,474	0	75%	0%
English-ParCorFull	19	543	10,798	0	6.1%	0.7%
French-Democrat	126	13,054	284,823	0	81.8%	0%
German-ParCorFull	19	543	10,602	0	5.8%	0.3%
German-PotsdamCC	176	2,238	33,222	0	76.5%	6.3%
Hungarian-SzegedKoref	400	8,820	123,976	4,849	7.9%	0.4%
Lithuanian-LCC	100	1,714	37,014	0	11.2%	0%
Polish-PCC	1828	35,874	538,891	864	82.6%	1.0%
Russian-RuCor	181	9,035	156,636	0	2.5%	0.5%
Spanish-AnCora	1635	17,662	517,258	8,111	73.4%	0%

Table 1: Dataset Statistics

Model	Pretrained params	New params
mBERT	180M	40M
XLM-R	350M	50M

Table 2: Number of trainable parameters of the models

where GOLD(i) is the set of spans in the training data that are antecedents.

The model achieves state-of-the-art performance on the OntoNotes dataset where singletons are not annotated. We believe the model is optimal for the CorefUD dataset as well since some of the datasets of the CorefUD do not contain singletons. Moreover, the evaluation metric ignores singletons, so it does not matter that the model is not able to predict them.

Employed Models We based our model on XLM Roberta large (Conneau et al., 2020), which is significantly larger than multilingual BERT (Devlin et al., 2018) used by the baseline. The number of parameters is provided in Table 2. We also tried to use the best monolingual model for each language.

Joined Model Pretraining As you can see from Table 2, there are approximately 50 million parameters trained from scratch for XLM-R. For smaller datasets, it is practically impossible to train so many random parameters. To solve this issue, we first pre-train the model on the joined dataset and then fine-tune the model for a specific language.

Heads Prediction As mentioned above, the official scorer uses min-span evaluation with head words as min spans. Because we do not know the rules used to select single mention head in the dataset, we decided to train to model to predict the heads instead of the whole spans to optimize the evaluation metric. Having all the useful information (even dependency trees), the model should learn the original rules for selecting the head.

The simplest way to predict the mention heads would be to simply represent mention with its head word on the input. But this is not an ideal solution since multiple mentions can have the same head. If we represented a mention with only the head, some mentions would be joined, and their clusters would be merged.

To avoid this, we represent mention with the whole span, and just at the top of our model, we predict the head of each mention and output only the head word(s). This way, the mentions are represented with their spans when we build the clusters, and the clusters of two different mentions with the same head are not merged as in the case of the simple approach mentioned above.

We implemented two versions of the head prediction model. Both are implemented as separate classification heads on the top of our coreference resolution model.

The first model predicts the relative position of the head word(s) inside a span using the hidden representation of the span from the CR model. Output probabilities of head positions are obtained using sigmoid activation so the model can predict multiple heads even though there is only single head word in the gold data. This is particular optimization of the evaluation metric: If there are more words likely to be a head word of the span, it is statistically better to output all of them.

The second model uses a binary classification of each span and head candidate pair, so again, there can be more head words of a single span predicted.

Trees We believe dependency information can help the model significantly, especially when manually annotated dependencies are provided (Czech PDT, for example). Moreover, the dependency information is necessary to find mention head.

To encode syntactic information, we add to each token representation its path to *ROOT* in the dependency tree. In more detail, we first set the maximum tree depth parameter and then concatenate Bert representations of all parents up to max depth with the embedding of the corresponding dependency relation. Thus the resulting tree structure representation has the size of $max\_tree\_depth \times (bert\_emb\_size + deprel\_emb\_size)$. This representation is then concatenated with bert embedding of each token.

3 Training

We trained all the models on NVIDIA A40 graphic cards using online learning (batch size 1 document). We limit the maximum sequence length to 6 non-overlapping segments of 512 tokens. During training, if the document is longer than 6×512 tokens, a random segment offset is sampled to take random continuous block of 6 segments, and the rest of them is discarded. During prediction, longer documents are split into independent sub-documents (for simplicity, non-overlapping again). We train a model for each dataset for approximately 80k updates in our monolingual experiments. For joined-pre-trained models, we use 80k steps for model pre-training on all the datasets and approximately 30k for fine-tunning on each dataset. Each training took from 8 to 20 hours.

4 Results & Discussion

Results of several variants of our model are presented in Table 3.

Monoling column shows the result of the monolingual model specific for each language. *XLM-R* column presents results of XLM Roberta large trained for each dataset separately. *Joined* is the joined model described in the Model section. The columns marked with + mean the best model from all to the left, with the additional feature. *+dev* means that the dev data part was added to training data, *+S2H* is the model with mention head prediction described earlier. Both methods for mention head prediction have statistically equal performance (we cannot tell which one is better). The reported numbers are for the first one. The results in column *+tree* correspond to adding the dependency structure as described.

It is not surprising that employing a larger model (XLMR-R large or monolingual) significantly improved the performance of the baseline. The results of the joined model are much more interesting. We can see that for some smaller datasets (e. g. German), the performance gain is huge. But if we have a look at Table 2, it makes sense because it is hard (or impossible) to train 50M parameters from scratch on a small dataset. It is also interesting that Polish is the only language where the monolingual model outperformed the joined model. But the reasons for this are probably straightforward. The polish dataset is one of the largest, so joined pre-training is not needed. Moreover there is a large monolingual model for Polish, so it is natural that it outperformed XLM-R large. For three datasets, there is a significant gain by employing mention head prediction. The difference should be even bigger when we add syntactic structure to the model. [2] Unfortunately, we did not manage to include this feature on time. From the results table, we can see that adding the trees does not help. In fact, it decreases performance significantly. We believe this is caused by some bug in our implementation, but we did not have enough time to correct it before the end of the competition.

4.1 Comparison To Other Systems

The comparison to other participating systems is shown in Table 4. Our system ended up in 3rd place. Surprisingly, although the winning system outperformed ours by a large margin on average, our system reached the best performance for two datasets (*german_parcor* and *hungarian*). It would be interesting to look at both systems' differences to find out why.

[2] The potential gain by outputting only mention heads can be found in Žabokrtský et al. (2022)

Dataset/Model	monolingual model name	reference	BASELINE	Monoling	XLM-R	joined	+dev	+S2H	+Tree
ca_ancora	PlanTL-GOB-ES/roberta-base-ca	(Armengol-Estapé et al., 2021)	63.74	69.61	66.19	68.81	**70.55**	69.91	68.32
cs_pcedt	Czert-B-base-cased	(Sido et al., 2021)	70	73.74	73.55	73.85	**74.07**	71.12	73.61
cs_pdt	Czert-B-base-cased	(Sido et al., 2021)	67.27	69.81	70.99	70.63	71.49	**72.42**	70.99
de_parcorfull	deepset/gbert-base	(Chan et al., 2020)	33.75	43.04	33.75	68.91	**73.9**	68.3	65.29
de_potsdamcc	deepset/gbert-large	(Chan et al., 2020)	55.44	58.81	59.03	**70.35**	66.02	68.68	67.35
en_gum	roberta-large	(Zhuang et al., 2021)	62.59	68	66.27	68.16	**68.31**	66.88	67.39
en_parcorfull	roberta-large	(Zhuang et al., 2021)	36.44	25.84	**36.44**	30.21	31.9	23.45	40.05
es_ancora	PlanTL-GOB-ES/roberta-large-bne	(Gutiérrez-Fandiño et al., 2022)	65.98	60.12	67.99	71.24	71.48	**72.32**	72.04
fr_democrat	camembert/camembert-large	(Martin et al., 2020)	55.55	56.76	55.94	59.8	60.12	**61.39**	60.03
hu_szegedkoref	SZTAKI-HLT/hubert-base-cc	(Nemeskey, 2021)	52.35	59.76	60.68	63.24	**65.01**	64.67	62.77
lt_lcc	EMBEDDIA/litlat-bert	(Ulčar and Robnik-Šikonja, 2021)	64.81	66.93	64.81	66.34	**68.05**	67.49	64.01
pl_pcc	allegro/herbert-large-cased	(Mroczkowski et al., 2021)	65.34	**75.2**	73.19	73.66	74.46	74.56	73.38
ru_rucor	DeepPavlov/rubert-base-cased	(Kuratov and Arkhipov, 2019)	67.66	69.33	**77.5**	75.5	74.82	76.02	75.94
avg			58.53	61.30	62.03	66.21	66.94	65.94	65.94

Table 3: Results

#	User	avg	ca	cs_pcedt	cs_pdt	de_pc	de_pots	en_gum	en_pc	es	fr	hu	lt_lcc	pl_pcc	ru
1	straka	**70.72**	78.18	**78.59**	**77.69**	65.52	70.69	72.5	**39**	**81.39**	**65.27**	63.15	**69.92**	78.12	**79.34**
2	straka-single-multil	69.56	**78.49**	78.49	77.57	59.94	**71.11**	**73.2**	33.55	80.8	64.35	63.38	67.38	**78.32**	77.74
3	**ours**	67.64	70.55	74.07	72.42	**73.9**	68.68	68.31	31.9	72.32	61.39	**65.01**	68.05	75.2	77.5
4	straka-single-data	64.3	76.34	77.87	76.76	36.5	56.65	70.66	23.48	78.78	64.94	62.94	61.32	73.36	76.26
5	berulasek	59.72	64.67	70.56	67.95	38.5	57.7	63.07	36.44	66.61	56.04	55.02	65.67	65.99	68.17
6	*BASELINE*	58.53	63.74	70	67.27	33.75	55.44	62.59	36.44	65.98	55.55	52.35	64.81	65.34	67.66
7	Moravec	55.05	58.25	68.19	64.71	31.86	52.84	59.15	36.44	62.01	54.87	52	59.49	63.4	52.49
8	simple_baseline	18.14	15.58	5.51	9.48	29.81	19.41	21.99	11.37	16.64	21.74	17	27.53	15.69	24.06
9	k-sap	5.9	0	0	0	0	0	0	0	0	0	0	0	76.67	0

Table 4: Comparison to Other Participating Systems

5 Conclusion

We successfully applied an end-to-end neural coreference resolution system to the CRAC 2022 shared task. There are two main outcomes of our work. **1)** Joined training helps a lot. Our experiments support the fulfillment of the goals of the CorefUD dataset to help the models by harmonizing the annotation schemas. **2)** For the official scoring metric, predicting only the mention heads increases performance. This means that syntactic structure helps to identify mentions. Of course, such evaluation is a bit artificial and does not reflect the real-world scenario, where we do not have the gold syntax. We also suggested injecting syntactic information into the model. Unfortunately, we did not manage to get any improvement with this approach. Our system ended up in 3rd place. Moreover, we reached the best performance on two datasets out of 13.

Acknowledgements

This work has been supported by Grant No. SGS-2022-016 Advanced methods of data processing and analysis. Computational resources were supplied by the project "e-Infrastruktura CZ" (e-INFRA CZ LM2018140) supported by the Ministry of Education, Youth and Sports of the Czech Republic.

References

Jordi Armengol-Estapé, Casimiro Pio Carrino, Carlos Rodriguez-Penagos, Ona de Gibert Bonet, Carme Armentano-Oller, Aitor Gonzalez-Agirre, Maite Melero, and Marta Villegas. 2021. Are multilingual models the best choice for moderately under-resourced languages? A comprehensive assessment for Catalan. In *Findings of the Association for Computational Linguistics: ACL-IJCNLP 2021*, pages 4933–4946, Online. Association for Computational Linguistics.

Branden Chan, Stefan Schweter, and Timo Möller. 2020. German's next language model. In *Proceedings of the 28th International Conference on Computational Linguistics*, pages 6788–6796.

Alexis Conneau, Kartikay Khandelwal, Naman Goyal, Vishrav Chaudhary, Guillaume Wenzek, Francisco Guzmán, Édouard Grave, Myle Ott, Luke Zettlemoyer, and Veselin Stoyanov. 2020. Unsupervised cross-lingual representation learning at scale. In *Proceedings of the 58th Annual Meeting of the Association for Computational Linguistics*, pages 8440–8451.

Jacob Devlin, Ming-Wei Chang, Kenton Lee, and Kristina Toutanova. 2018. BERT: pre-training of deep bidirectional transformers for language understanding. *CoRR*, abs/1810.04805.

Asier Gutiérrez-Fandiño, Jordi Armengol-Estapé, Marc Pàmies, Joan Llop-Palao, Joaquin Silveira-Ocampo, Casimiro Pio Carrino, Carme Armentano-Oller, Carlos Rodriguez-Penagos, Aitor Gonzalez-Agirre, and

Marta Villegas. 2022. Maria: Spanish language models. *Procesamiento del Lenguaje Natural*, 68(0):39–60.

Yuri Kuratov and Mikhail Arkhipov. 2019. Adaptation of deep bidirectional multilingual transformers for russian language. *arXiv preprint arXiv:1905.07213*.

Kenton Lee, Luheng He, Mike Lewis, and Luke Zettlemoyer. 2017. End-to-end neural coreference resolution. In *Proceedings of the 2017 Conference on Empirical Methods in Natural Language Processing*, pages 188–197, Copenhagen, Denmark. Association for Computational Linguistics.

Louis Martin, Benjamin Muller, Pedro Javier Ortiz Suárez, Yoann Dupont, Laurent Romary, Éric Villemonte de la Clergerie, Djamé Seddah, and Benoît Sagot. 2020. Camembert: a tasty french language model. In *ACL 2020-58th Annual Meeting of the Association for Computational Linguistics*.

Robert Mroczkowski, Piotr Rybak, Alina Wróblewska, and Ireneusz Gawlik. 2021. HerBERT: Efficiently pretrained transformer-based language model for Polish. In *Proceedings of the 8th Workshop on Balto-Slavic Natural Language Processing*, pages 1–10, Kiyv, Ukraine. Association for Computational Linguistics.

Anna Nedoluzhko, Michal Novák, Martin Popel, Zdeněk Žabokrtskỳ, Amir Zeldes, and Daniel Zeman. 2022. Corefud 1.0: Coreference meets universal dependencies. In *Proceedings of LREC*.

Anna Nedoluzhko, Michal Novák, Martin Popel, Zdeněk Žabokrtský, and Daniel Zeman. 2021. *Coreference meets Universal Dependencies – a pilot experiment on harmonizing coreference datasets for 11 languages*. ÚFAL MFF UK, Praha, Czechia.

Dávid Márk Nemeskey. 2021. Introducing `huBERT`. In *XVII. Magyar Számítógépes Nyelvészeti Konferencia (MSZNY2021)*, page TBA, Szeged.

Ondřej Pražák, Miloslav Konopík, and Jakub Sido. 2021. Multilingual coreference resolution with harmonized annotations. In *Proceedings of the International Conference on Recent Advances in Natural Language Processing (RANLP 2021)*, pages 1119–1123.

Jakub Sido, Ondřej Pražák, Pavel Přibáň, Jan Pašek, Michal Seják, and Miloslav Konopík. 2021. Czert–czech bert-like model for language representation. In *Proceedings of the International Conference on Recent Advances in Natural Language Processing (RANLP 2021)*, pages 1326–1338.

Rhea Sukthanker, Soujanya Poria, Erik Cambria, and Ramkumar Thirunavukarasu. 2020. Anaphora and coreference resolution: A review. *Information Fusion*, 59:139–162.

Matej Ulčar and Marko Robnik-Šikonja. 2021. Training dataset and dictionary sizes matter in bert models: the case of baltic languages. *arXiv preprint arXiv:2112.10553*.

Liu Zhuang, Lin Wayne, Shi Ya, and Zhao Jun. 2021. A robustly optimized bert pre-training approach with post-training. In *Proceedings of the 20th Chinese National Conference on Computational Linguistics*, pages 1218–1227.

Zdeněk Žabokrtský, Miloslav Konopík, Anna Nedoluzhko, Michal Novák, Maciej Ogrodniczuk, Martin Popel, Ondřej Pražák, Jakub Sido, Daniel Zeman, and Yilun Zhu. 2022. Findings of the shared task on multilingual coreference resolution. In *Proceedings of the Fifth Workshop on Computational Models of Reference, Anaphora and Coreference*, Gyeongju, Republic of Korea. Association for Computational Linguistics.

ÚFAL CorPipe at CRAC 2022: Effectivity of Multilingual Models for Coreference Resolution

Milan Straka and **Jana Straková**
Charles University, Faculty of Mathematics and Physics
Institute of Formal and Applied Lingustics
Malostranské nám. 25, Prague, Czech Republic
straka,strakova@ufal.mff.cuni.cz

Abstract

We describe the winning submission to the CRAC 2022 Shared Task on Multilingual Coreference Resolution. Our system first solves mention detection and then coreference linking on the retrieved spans with an antecedent-maximization approach, and both tasks are fine-tuned jointly with shared Transformer weights. We report results of fine-tuning a wide range of pretrained models. The center of this contribution are fine-tuned multilingual models. We found one large multilingual model with sufficiently large encoder to increase performance on all datasets across the board, with the benefit not limited only to the underrepresented languages or groups of typologically relative languages. The source code is available at `https://github.com/ufal/crac2022-corpipe`.

1 Introduction

Coreference resolution is a task of identifying and clustering multiple occurrences of entities across a textual document. The CRAC 2022 Shared Task on Multilingual Coreference Resolution (Žabokrtský et al., 2022) features coreference resolution on 13 datasets in 10 languages, originating from the CorefUD 1.0 multilingual dataset (Nedoluzhko et al., 2021, 2022).

Coreference resolution is often divided into two subtasks, *mention detection* and *coreference linking* (also *clustering*). Our contribution solves these tasks neither as a purely pipeline approach with two separate sequential models, nor as an end-to-end system (Lee et al., 2017, 2018), as is recently more common (e.g., the baseline; Pražák et al., 2021), but somewhere in between: We first solve mention detection and then coreference linking with an antecedent-maximization algorithm, but both tasks are jointly fine-tuned in one shared large language model. This circumvents the explosion of possible spans in an end-to-end approach, allows for a single retrieval of mentions only, while keeping the benefit of sharing the weights and training only one model for two highly related tasks (contribution 1).

Our architecture is a fine-tuned large language model, with experimental results leaning toward large pretrained models with better multilingual representation. We experimented with a wide range of pretrained language models (Devlin et al., 2019; Conneau et al., 2020; Chung et al., 2021; Armengol-Estapé et al., 2021; Straka et al., 2021; Chan et al., 2020; Devlin et al., 2019; Joshi et al., 2020; Cañete et al., 2020; Martin et al., 2020; Nemeskey, 2020; Ulčar and Robnik-Šikonja, 2021; Mroczkowski et al., 2021; Kuratov and Arkhipov, 2019), of which RemBERT (Chung et al., 2021) proved the most effective (contribution 2).

We found *multilingual models* at the center of our research attention in the CRAC 2022 Shared Task. The shared task featured datasets with sizes ranging from tiny (457 training sentences in `de` and `en parcorfull`) to relatively large (nearly 40K training sentences in `cs pcedt` and `cs pdt`), all of them evaluated with equal weight (macro average). This implied that special care must be devoted to leveling the performance on all datasets. We experimented with various combinations of fine-tuned multilingual models and various sampling strategies. Although our motivation was to mitigate the poor performance on smaller specimens, we surprisingly found that one large multilingual model with sufficiently large encoder improves results on all datasets, not only the small or linguistically related ones (contribution 3).

To sum up, our contributions are the following:

1. We present a jointly trained pipeline approach for coreference resolution.
2. Although many monolingual base models surpass their multilingual base counterparts, in the end, one large multilingual pretrained model gives the best performance over base, albeit specifically pretrained monolingual encoders.

Proceedings of the CRAC 2022 Shared Task on Multilingual Coreference Resolution, pages 28–37
October 17, 2022

3. One fine-tuned all-data multilingual model with sufficiently large encoder outperforms individual models across all datasets, not only the smaller or typologically related ones.

The source code of our system is available at `https://github.com/ufal/crac2022-corpipe`.

2 Related Work

Coreference resolution is often divided into two subtasks: *mention detection* and *coreference linking* (or *clustering*). These can be solved either separately (pipeline approach) or, more recently, in an end-to-end fashion (Lee et al., 2017, 2018). Such was also the approach of the baseline (Pražák et al., 2021). Our proposal takes what we hope is advantageous from both approaches: We solve both tasks sequentially, but the weights are trained jointly in a shared network.

As in all other NLP areas, deep learning with representations from large language models represents the current state-of-the-art (Kantor and Globerson, 2019; Joshi et al., 2019, 2020). We build on these works which use BERT (Devlin et al., 2019) by comparing BERT with its successors, the language-specific mutations of BERT (Armengol-Estapé et al., 2021; Straka et al., 2021; Chan et al., 2020; Devlin et al., 2019; Joshi et al., 2020; Cañete et al., 2020; Martin et al., 2020; Nemeskey, 2020; Ulčar and Robnik-Šikonja, 2021; Mroczkowski et al., 2021; Kuratov and Arkhipov, 2019), and multilingual variants: mBERT (Devlin et al., 2019), XLM-R base and XLM-R large (Conneau et al., 2020), and RemBERT (Chung et al., 2021).

There are mixed accounts in the literature on globally decoding the entities (clusters) via higher-order methods. Kantor and Globerson (2019) improved state-of-the-art on the CoNLL-2012 shared task with differentiable end-to-end manner enabling higher-order inference: mentions are represented as the sum of all mentions of the entity (*entity equalization*). Other higher-order coreference linking methods include *attended antecedent* (Lee et al., 2018; Fei et al., 2019; Joshi et al., 2019, 2020). On the other hand, Xu and Choi (2020) thoroughly investigated the contribution of higher-order methods to the models performance and conclude that with modern encoders, higher-order methods contribute only marginally or negatively. As we model *all* antecedent links during training in a dot-product attention matrix, we inherently "equalize" entities, although not with an explicit algorithm.

3 Methods

An overview of the model architecture is shown in Figure 1. In the following sections, we describe the components of the model in detail, with reference to the corresponding parts of Figure 1.

3.1 Architecture

We consider that the enumeration of all possible spans as mention candidates in an end-to-end approach, despite aggressive pruning, may lead to explosion of options and possibly harm the coreference linking because the candidate set is heavily biased toward negative outcome: only a fraction of the spans is an actual mention and of these, only a fraction is a mention of the same entity. Furthermore, this approach does not allow the retrieval of mentions only. Hence, we propose a jointly trained, pipeline approach: we first solve *mention detection* and then *coreference linking* only on the retrieved mentions. However, to share the information between these highly related tasks and to keep a single model, we fine-tune one shared large language model, only with separately stacked hidden layers on top of the shared large language model for each task. In Figure 1, the orange box corresponds to the shared fine-tuned large language model (encoder), the green box corresponds to the *mention detection* task and the purple box corresponds to the *coreference linking* task.

In all fairness it should be said that we did not experimentally compare our architecture with the purely pipeline models with separate encoders nor the end-to-end approach, as pursuing three architectures to final submission was beyond our means in the given time frame. We venture to suggest that separately trained pipeline models might have the advantage of greater capacity (separate large language model for each task) but might become expensive as both models must be separately fine-tuned and hyperparameter-searched.

3.2 Token Representations (Encoder)

Each token receives a contextualized representation from the encoder, a vector of dimension D ($D = 768$ for base encoders, $D = 1024$ for XLM-R large, $D = 1152$ for RemBERT). The retrieval of contextualized token representation corresponds to the orange box in the bottom of Figure 1. The representation is shared between the *mention detection* and *coreference linking* tasks.

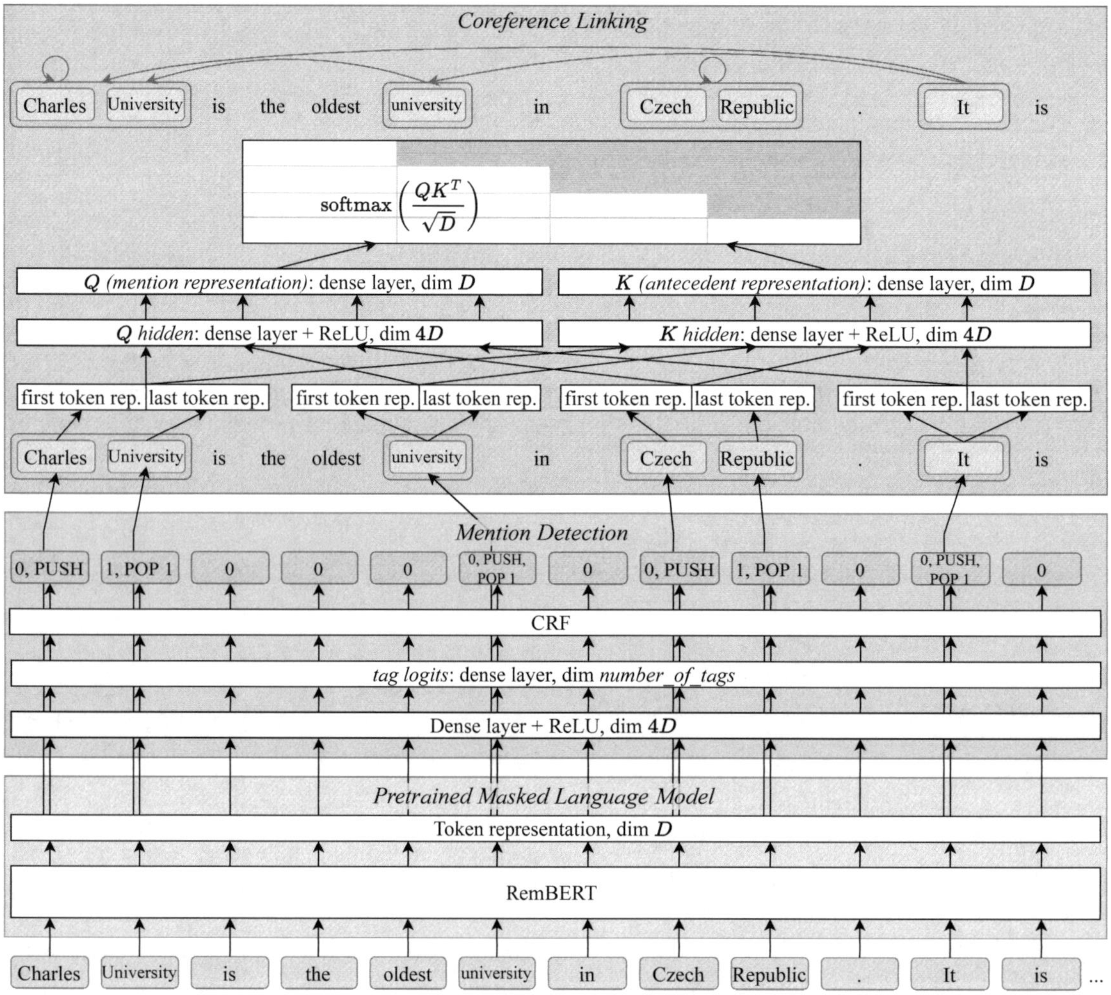

Figure 1: CorPipe model architecture. Best viewed in color.

We experimented with the following pretrained multilingual language models:

- RemBERT (Chung et al., 2021),
- XLM-R base and large (Conneau et al., 2020),
- mBERT (Devlin et al., 2019),

and the following published language-specific models:[1]

- Catalan BERTa (Armengol-Estapé et al., 2021),
- Czech RoBERTa RobeCzech (Straka et al., 2021),
- German gBERT (Chan et al., 2020),
- English SpanBERT (Joshi et al., 2020),
- Spanish BETO (Cañete et al., 2020),
- French CamemBERT (Martin et al., 2020),
- Hungarian HuBERT (Nemeskey, 2020),
- Lithuanian LitLatBERT (Ulčar and Robnik-Šikonja, 2021),
- Polish HerBERT (Mroczkowski et al., 2021),
- Russian RuBERT (Kuratov and Arkhipov, 2019).

[1]For each language, we present the monolingual model that worked best in our settings, if more exist.

3.3 Empty Nodes

Some dependency grammar annotation schools allow, or even require, the so-called *empty nodes*, which are superficial nodes of a dependency graph unseen on the surface level, i.e., not directly corresponding to any surface token of the sentence. The empty nodes usually account for ellipsis, such as in a sentence *"Mary likes roses and John (likes) violets."*, in which the verb "likes" is omitted but depending on the annotation guidelines may be reconstructed in the dependency tree. These nodes may carry coreference annotation, and they very often do in pro-drop languages (like Slavic or Romance languages). In Czech example: *"Řekl, že nepřijde."*, translated as *"(He) said that (he) won't come."*, both pronouns are dropped but implied by the morphology of the verb.

To allow the empty nodes, if occurring, to be naturally represented on the input and the output of the fine-tuned model and be part of the fine-tuning, we simply draw them to the surface, that is, we create a new token occupying the implied position of the artificial empty node and assign whatever text that was annotated with it (or none).[2] To recognize such artificial tokens from regular tokens, we prepend an artificial special character to any such token originating from an empty-node.

3.4 Mention Detection

We model mention detection as a sequence token-level classification problem, which considers a sequence of tokens on the input and a corresponding sequence of tags on the output. The proposed tags are an extension of BIO encoding, which in addition can handle embedded and also overlapping mention spans. Each tag is a sequence of the following stack manipulation instructions:

- $0..N$ `POP` instructions, each closing a mention from the stack. To handle crossing mention spans, the instruction has a parameter specifying which mention to close using its index from the top of the stack. The most frequently used value is 1 (the top of the stack), because closing the mention on the top of the stack is sufficient to encode arbitrarily embedded non-crossing mention spans.
- $0..N$ `PUSH` instructions, each starting a new mention on the top of the stack.
- $0..N$ `POP` instructions again, each closing a single-token mention started by a previous `PUSH` in the same step. We could represent such single-word mentions using specialized `UNIT` instructions instead of a `PUSH-POP` pair, but we opted for less instructions for the simplicity of the decoder.

The above mentioned stack instructions are concatenated into a single tag, predicted by a classifier as one label per token.

Because not all sequences of tags are valid (i.e., we are performing structured prediction), we process the tags by a linear-chain CRF. Finally, in order to allow the CRF to check whether there is a mention to be closed by a `POP` instruction, we include the size of the stack in the tag.[3]

The mention detection classifier corresponds to the green box in Figure 1. Token representation of dimension D is processed by a hidden ReLU layer of dimension $4D$, then by a linear layer producing tag logits, and finally by a CRF layer.

3.5 Coreference Linking

We approach coreference linking by considering, for each mention, a probability distribution of the preceding mentions in the previous context (more on context window in Section 3.6) being antecedents of the current mention. We also include the mention itself in the distribution, and consider it a technical antecedent if the mention has no antecedents.

During training, our goal is to predict *all* mention antecedents using a categorical cross-entropy loss. During prediction, however, we predict only the most probable antecedent for every mention, noting that any correct antecedent results in the same coreference cluster.[4]

The computation of the antecedent distribution, corresponding to the purple box in Figure 1, starts by constructing an initial representation of every mention by concatenating the token representations of its first and last tokens.[5] Using this representation, we compute Q (the representation of a reference candidate) and K (the representation of an antecedent candidate), both using a hidden ReLU layer with dimensionality $4D$ followed by a bias-free linear layer of dimensionality D. Finally, we compute the antecedent distribution using masked dot-product self-attention (Vaswani et al., 2017).

The inclusion of "self" in the pool of antecedents naturally allows for the so-called *singletons*, which are mentions without antecedent (entities mentioned only once, for example "Czech Republic" in Figure 1). Singletons were excluded from the

[2] We use the form associated with a given empty node; if empty, we fall back to the (possibly empty) lemma.

[3] Our approach does not handle discontinuous mentions. While we could support them by introducing an instruction continuing an already closed span, handling discontinuous mentions would also require support in the mention encoder.

[4] This is true only when considering previous mentions as antecedents; if we considered both previous and following mentions as antecedents, disconnected components of a single coreference cluster could be formed.

[5] Such an approach assumes the mentions are continuous. We handle discontinuous mentions by limiting them to their largest continuous sub-span containing the syntactic head of the mention (see Section 3.8).

official evaluation primary metric, but the official evaluation with singletons on the test set and the ablation experiments with singletons on the dev set can be found in Section 4.6.

The fact that during training a reference should recognize all its antecedents might seem inconsistent with the inference regime, where only a single most probable antecedent is retrieved. We therefore demonstrate the effectiveness of considering all antecedents by also evaluating a strategy of limiting the number of gold antecedents to at most 1, 2, or 3 previous ones (***At most 1 link***, ***At most 2 links*** or ***At most 3 links***) in Section 4.5.

3.6 Context Window

For each sentence, we consider a sliding context of 512 tokens, aligning the end of the current sentence towards the end of the window to allow for a larger left (past) context than the right (future) context. We experiment with several settings of the size of the right context in Section 4.4:

- ***Right context 0***: The end of the current sentence is perfectly aligned with the context of 512 tokens (no right context).
- ***Right context 50***: We leave 50 tokens for the right (future) context after the sentence end and whatever remains is the left (past) context; if there is not enough left context to fill the whole window of 512 tokens (e.g., the first sentence of the document), we increase the size of the right context to fill all the 512 tokens.
- ***Right context 100***: Same as before, but 100 tokens for the right context.

Unless stated otherwise, we use right context of 50.

3.7 Multilingual Models

We introduced *multilinguality* as our natural research interest of CRAC 2022 Shared Task. We experimented with various combinations of models with respect to size and/or language, and in the end, we submitted three contributions to the final evaluation:

- ***individual***: The models were fine-tuned using solely the training data of the corresponding dataset.[6]
- ***multilingual***: All training data were used for fine-tuning a single multilingual model, with examples sampled according to the logarithm of the individual dataset sizes. The final checkpoint of the last training epoch was used for prediction, so there is only one single large model for all datasets, an option which could most easily qualify as a deliverable software product for multilingual coreference resolution.
- ***best dev***: In this setting we considered, for every dataset, the test set prediction corresponding to a model and optimum epoch achieving the best development set performance. An intuition behind this decision is that in the multilingual settings, the smaller datasets converge sooner, while the large ones need more iterations. This is supported by the seemingly linear relationship between the logarithm of the number of training sentences and the optimum number of training epochs in Figure 2.

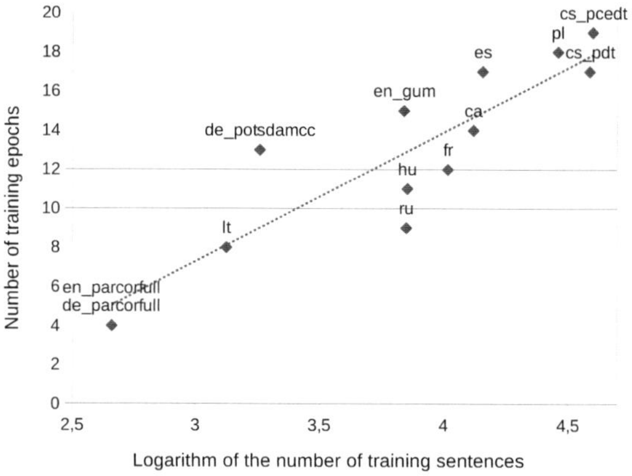

Figure 2: Dependency of the number of the optimum training epochs on the logarithm of the corpus size.

When mixing multilingual data, sampling ratios of the datasets must be determined. We experimented with three strategies for sampling the datasets; the examples are then always sampled uniformly from the chosen dataset:

- ***logarithmic***: Datasets are sampled with the probability reflecting the logarithm of their size.[7]
- ***uniform***: Datasets are sampled with uniform probability.
- ***linear***: Datasets are sampled in proportion linear to their size, which effectively equals to sampling the examples uniformly from the concatenation of the datasets.

[6]With the exception of `de` and `en parcorfull` – these corpora are extremely small (457 sentences each) and translations of each other, so we always train on a concatenation of them when finetuning an individual language model.

[7]We scaled the logarithmic sampling rations to the range 1 to 5, and rounded them for convenience.

Finally, dataset labels (corpus ids) may or may not be be added to the input to discriminate the origins. We call these settings ***w/ corpus id*** and ***w/o corpus id***.

We compare all the above mentioned strategies for creating multilingual models in Section 4.1.

3.8 Limiting Mention Spans to Their Heads

The official CRAC 2022 Shared Task evaluation relied on the lenient *partial matching*, which considers mention span correctly detected if it contains the syntactic head of the gold mention and at the same time, the predicted mention span does not include any tokens outside the gold mention span. Hence it seems prudent to not "overpredict" too long mention spans and prune the predicted mention spans to their syntactic head, given that syntactic analysis is available in the data. We show ablation results including the full mention spans in Section 4.7.

3.9 Training

We trained our models using a lazy variant of the Adam optimizer (Kingma and Ba, 2015), with a batch size of 8. The *base* variants were fine-tuned on a single 16GB GeForce/Quadro GPU, using a slanted triangular learning rate schedule – first linearly increasing from 0 to $2 \cdot 10^{-5}$ in the first 10% of the training, and then linearly decaying to 0 at the end of the training. The multilingual models were trained for 30 epochs, each consisting of 6000 batches; the individual models were trained for up to 100 epochs depending on dataset size.

The *large* models required fine-tuning on two 25GB GeForce GPUs, the peak learning rate was 10^{-5} , the multilingual models were trained for 20 epochs and the individual models up to 50 epochs. We trained 8 large multilingual models (each taking 42 hours), considering both XLM-R large and RemBERT, uniform and logarithmic mixing, presence of corpus id, and $\beta_2 = 0.99$ in addition to the default one. The best-performing model uses RemBERT, logarithmic mixing without corpus id, and default β_2.

4 Results

Official results of the CRAC 2022 Shared Task on the test set can be found in Table 1. Our multilingual models, ***best dev*** and ***multilingual***, scored 1st and 2nd, respectively, while our ***individual*** models trained on each dataset placed 4th.

4.1 Multilingual Models

A view on the effectiveness of multilingual models is shown in official ablation results on test data in Table 2, which compares all our three individual/multilingual settings: ***multilingual*** as a baseline, ***individual*** and ***best dev***, using a base encoder (XLM-R base for the multilingual baseline, best-performing base encoder for the remaining cases) and a large encoder (RemBERT). The ***multilingual*** is superior to ***individual*** for all datasets, with the exception of the three largest datasets using a base encoder – we hypothesize that the base encoder does not have sufficient capacity to capture the largest datasets in the ***multilingual*** setting, because with a large encoder, also the three largest datasets benefit from the ***multilingual*** model. Furthermore, Table 4.C demonstrates that while XLM-R large is the best in the ***individual*** settings, RemBERT delivers superior ***multilingual*** performance.

Motivated by the improvements of the multilingual models, we considered a setting where 50% of the training data comes from a single dataset and the rest from all other datasets (with logarithmic mixing). Surprisingly, such setting delivers consistently worse performance than the multilingual models (last line of Table 4.C).

The comparison of ***logarithmic***, ***uniform***, and ***linear*** mixing, together with the presence or absence of ***corpus id***, is evaluated in Table 4.D and Table 4.E. Unexpectedly, neither the mixing rations nor the ***corpus id*** have a large effect on the results, which is surprising especially for the ***linear*** mixing, where the smallest treebanks are nearly 100 times less frequent than the largest one.

4.2 Zero-shot Evaluation

The prospect of not including the corpus id opens an interesting possibility of using the model in zero-shot setting, i.e., on a different language than it was trained on. To perform such zero-shot evaluation, we trained for every language a multilingual model *without* datasets in this language, and then evaluated the model on them. The results, presented in Table 4.F, were below our expectations, slightly surpassing 60% macro average on the development set with the RemBERT model.

4.3 Monolingual Pretrained Language Models

Table 4.G presents the evaluation of the best-performing monolingual base-sized pretrained models we found. While the specialized models

Team/Submission	Avg	ca	cs pcedt	cs pdt	de parc	de pots	en gum	en parc	es	fr	hu	lt	pl	ru
ÚFAL CorPipe	**70.72**	78.18	**78.59**	**77.69**	65.52	70.69	72.50	**39.00**	**81.39**	**65.27**	63.15	**69.92**	78.12	**79.34**
best dev	**1**	2	**1**	**1**	2	2	2	**1**	**1**	**1**	3	**1**	2	**1**
ÚFAL CorPipe	69.56	**78.49**	78.49	77.57	59.94	**71.11**	**73.20**	33.55	80.80	64.35	63.38	67.38	**78.32**	77.74
multilingual	2	**1**	2	2	3	**1**	**1**	3	2	3	2	3	**1**	2
UWB	67.64	70.55	74.07	72.42	**73.90**	68.68	68.31	31.90	72.32	61.39	**65.01**	68.05	75.20	77.50
ondfa†	3	4	4	4	**1**	3	4	4	4	4	**1**	2	4	3
ÚFAL CorPipe	64.30	76.34	77.87	76.76	36.50	56.65	70.66	23.48	78.78	64.94	62.94	61.32	73.36	76.26
individual	4	3	3	3	5	5	3	5	3	2	4	6	5	4
Barbora Dohnalová	59.72	64.67	70.56	67.95	38.50	57.70	63.07	36.44	66.61	56.04	55.02	65.67	65.99	68.17
berulasek	5	5	5	5	4	4	5	2	5	5	5	4	6	5
UWB	58.53	63.74	70.00	67.27	33.75	55.44	62.59	36.44	65.98	55.55	52.35	64.81	65.34	67.66
BASELINE‡	6	6	6	6	6	6	6	2	6	6	6	5	7	6
Matouš Moravec	55.05	58.25	68.19	64.71	31.86	52.84	59.15	36.44	62.01	54.87	52.00	59.49	63.40	52.49
moravec	7	7	7	7	7	7	7	2	7	7	7	7	8	7

Table 1: Official results of CRAC 2022 Shared Task on the test set (CoNLL score in %). The systems † and ‡ are described in Pražák and Konopik (2022) and Pražák et al. (2021), respectively; the rest in Žabokrtský et al. (2022).

Experiment	Avg	ca	cs pcedt	cs pdt	de parc	de pots	en gum	en parc	es	fr	hu	lt	pl	ru
XLM-R base, multilingual	67.8	77.1	75.8	74.3	54.7	66.9	70.1	38.5	77.6	64.2	62.3	69.4	73.3	76.6
Best base model, individual	-5.2	-4.0	+1.5	+2.2	-18.2	-9.8	-3.4	-15.0	-2.4	-2.4	-2.0	-8.1	+0.0	-5.6
Best base model, best dev	+0.4	-0.6	+1.5	+2.2	+2.0	+0.6	-1.0	-0.9	+1.2	-1.1	+0.6	+0.4	+0.0	+0.2
RemBERT, multilingual	+1.8	**+1.4**	+2.6	+3.3	+5.2	**+4.2**	**+3.1**	-4.9	+3.2	+0.1	**+1.1**	-2.0	**+5.0**	+1.1
RemBERT, individual	-3.5	-0.7	+2.0	+2.5	-18.2	-10.3	+0.6	-15.0	+1.2	+0.7	+0.7	-8.1	+0.0	-0.4
RemBERT, best dev	**+3.0**	+1.1	**+2.7**	**+3.4**	**+10.8**	+3.8	+2.4	**+0.5**	**+3.8**	**+1.0**	+0.9	**+0.5**	+4.8	**+2.7**

Table 2: Official results of ablation experiments on the test set (CoNLL score in %).

Team/Submission	Avg. with singletons
ÚFAL CorPipe, *best dev*	**72.98**
ÚFAL CorPipe, *multilingual*	71.81
ÚFAL CorPipe, *individual*	67.93
UWB, *ondfa*	58.06
Barbora Dohnalová, *berulasek*	50.84
UWB, BASELINE	49.69
Matouš Moravec, *moravec*	46.79

Table 3: Official results of evaluation with singletons on the test set.

consistently surpass mBERT and are mostly better than XLM-R base, they are all worse than the individual XLM-R large models (with the exception of Lithuanian) and even more dominated by the RemBERT multilingual model. This indicates that, nowadays, pretraining a base-sized monolingual BERT model has merit only in improving the running time, not model performance, when large pretrained multilingual models are now available.

4.4 Context Window

Table 4.H shows the effect of using a right context of size 0, 50, and 100. The evaluation, performed on a base-sized model with a preliminary, development version of CorPipe, shows that the presence of the right context is beneficial, but does not clearly indicate whether context of size 100 is better than 50.

4.5 Number of Links

The effect of limiting the number of predicted antecedents during training is presented by Table 4.I. The evaluation (performed again on a base-sized model with a preliminary, development version of CorPipe) shows that performance increases with the number of antecedents considered during training.

4.6 Singletons

Singletons (entities with only one mention in the document) were excluded from the official evaluation primary metric. Our antecedent-maximization strategy however accounts for them by adding "self" to antecedent candidates pool. We publish the official evaluation with singletons on the test set in Table 3 and the ablation evaluation with singletons on the dev set in Table 4.B.

Experiment	Avg	ca	cs pcedt	cs pdt	de parc	de pots	en gum	en parc	es	fr	hu	lt	pl	ru
A) The Effect of Using Full Mentions Instead of Only Their Heads														
CorPipe multilingual	73.2	76.9	79.3	78.1	70.6	74.7	74.8	61.2	80.9	67.4	64.6	76.0	75.2	71.4
+ full mentions	-1.8	-2.4	-1.2	-0.9	-3.0	-2.1	-1.7	-3.0	-2.6	-1.1	-1.8	-1.3	-1.2	-1.2
CorPipe individual	71.1	76.3	78.7	76.9	65.7	62.0	73.8	63.2	79.5	66.8	64.8	73.4	71.7	69.9
+ full mentions	+0.3	-1.9	-0.7	+0.2	+1.9	+10.6	-0.7	-5.0	-1.3	-0.5	-1.9	+1.3	+2.3	+0.3
CorPipe best dev	**76.0**	**78.1**	**79.5**	**78.5**	**73.9**	**78.3**	**76.0**	**75.1**	**81.8**	**69.0**	**69.2**	**78.0**	**76.3**	**74.6**
+ full mentions	-4.6	-3.6	-1.4	-1.3	-6.3	-5.6	-3.0	-16.9	-3.5	-2.6	-6.3	-3.3	-2.4	-4.4
B) Evaluation Including Singletons														
CorPipe multilingual	74.8	82.3	78.0	74.5	68.7	79.8	82.2	52.1	85.1	76.6	63.3	73.7	84.2	69.5
CorPipe individual	73.7	82.4	77.2	73.4	63.4	71.7	82.2	60.6	84.1	76.4	62.5	71.3	82.2	67.8
CorPipe best dev	**77.5**	**83.2**	**78.0**	**74.7**	**70.4**	**82.6**	**83.2**	**71.6**	**85.8**	**77.5**	**66.8**	**74.8**	**84.7**	**73.0**
C) Effect of Multilingual Data and the Pretrained Model														
XLM-R base multilingual	73.3	75.8	76.0	75.0	73.4	74.1	73.1	**75.4**	78.4	66.1	65.2	**78.0**	72.1	71.7
XLM-R large multilingual	+1.5	**+1.7**	+1.8	+2.0	+0.3	**+4.1**	+2.1	-4.5	+2.2	+1.7	+3.1	-0.0	+2.9	+0.9
RemBERT multilingual	**+1.9**	+1.6	**+3.3**	**+3.3**	**+2.9**	+2.4	**+2.4**	-6.1	**+2.7**	**+2.0**	**+4.0**	-1.2	**+3.7**	**+2.9**
XLM-R base individual	-4.6	-4.4	-0.3	-1.1	-7.8	-12.1	-1.9	-12.2	-2.8	-3.0	-3.8	-4.6	-2.3	-6.1
XLM-R large individual	-0.6	+0.2	+2.8	+3.0	-7.7	-5.2	-0.9	-4.4	+1.0	+0.3	+3.7	-5.4	+3.5	-1.2
RemBERT individual	-4.7	+0.6	+2.8	+1.9	-23.0	-12.1	+0.7	-30.5	+1.1	+0.7	-0.4	-8.9	+2.7	-1.8
RemBERT 50% additional	+0.3	+1.0	+2.5	+2.4	-1.4	-0.5	+1.7	-8.3	+0.9	+1.3	+1.6	-3.5	+3.6	+1.7
D) Effect of Mixing Ratios using XLM-R base Pretrained Model														
Logarithmic, w/o corpus id	**73.3**	75.8	76.0	75.0	**73.4**	**74.1**	**73.1**	**75.4**	78.4	66.1	65.2	78.0	72.1	**71.7**
Logarithmic, w/ corpus id	-0.4	-0.5	+0.1	+0.3	-0.8	-0.3	-0.6	-4.6	**+0.1**	**+0.6**	**+1.3**	-0.9	**+0.3**	-0.7
Uniform, w/o corpus id	-0.8	-0.5	-0.2	-0.9	-1.8	-3.5	-0.2	-1.9	+0.0	-0.0	+0.4	-1.1	+0.0	-1.5
Uniform, w/ corpus id	-1.6	-1.1	-0.5	-0.6	-6.4	-2.1	-0.4	-7.0	+0.1	+0.1	-0.5	-1.1	-0.6	-1.2
Linear, w/o corpus id	-0.3	**+0.1**	**+0.8**	**+1.1**	-1.1	-0.5	-0.5	-3.5	-0.1	+0.3	+1.0	**+0.3**	-0.1	-1.6
E) Effect of Mixing Ratios using RemBERT Pretrained Model														
Logarithmic, w/o corpus id	75.3	77.4	79.3	78.3	76.3	76.5	75.5	69.3	81.1	68.1	**69.2**	76.8	75.8	**74.6**
Logarithmic, w/ corpus id	**+0.6**	+0.4	+0.1	+0.1	**+3.0**	**+1.2**	-0.1	**+5.8**	+0.3	**+0.9**	-2.4	-1.3	+0.1	-0.2
Uniform, w/o corpus id	+0.1	+1.2	-0.3	-0.1	+2.4	+0.5	**+0.0**	-0.9	-0.1	+0.7	-0.6	-0.2	**+0.1**	-1.2
Uniform, w/ corpus id	-0.1	-0.0	-0.2	-0.3	-4.2	+0.3	-0.1	+4.5	+0.4	+0.6	-1.0	-0.1	+0.1	-1.2
Linear, w/o corpus id	-0.1	**+1.3**	**+0.1**	**+0.2**	-2.3	-0.5	-1.5	+1.9	**+0.5**	+0.7	-1.0	**+0.4**	+0.0	-1.3
F) Zero-shot Evaluation of a Multilingual Model														
Multilingual XLM-R base	73.3	75.8	76.0	75.0	73.4	74.1	73.1	**75.4**	78.4	66.1	65.2	**78.0**	72.1	71.7
Zero-shot XLM-R base	-17.1	-11.1	-28.6	-23.8	-13.3	-13.8	-19.8	-18.5	-6.8	-7.6	-16.1	-23.8	-24.6	-15.1
Multilingual RemBERT	**+1.9**	**+1.6**	**+3.3**	**+3.3**	**+2.9**	**+2.4**	**+2.4**	-6.1	**+2.7**	**+2.0**	**+4.0**	-1.2	**+3.7**	**+2.9**
Zero-shot RemBERT	-12.5	-6.7	-23.7	-20.6	-11.1	-7.5	-15.6	-9.8	-2.8	-8.3	-10.5	-20.0	-18.3	-7.2
G) Effect of Several Language-specific base Pretrained Models														
XLM-R base individual	68.7	71.4	75.7	73.9	65.7	62.0	71.2	63.2	75.6	63.1	61.5	73.4	69.8	65.6
mBERT (Devlin et al., 2019)	-2.8	-1.5	-3.0	-3.4	-3.3	+0.4	-2.8	-1.1	-1.8	-1.1	-2.7	-7.5	-4.4	-3.6
BERTa (Armengol-Estapé et al., 2021)		+1.3												
RobeCzech (Straka et al., 2021)			+2.0	+2.8										
gBERT (Chan et al., 2020)					-9.9	+5.3								
SpanBERT (Joshi et al., 2020)							-0.4	-2.4						
BETO (Cañete et al., 2020)									+0.4					
CamemBERT (Martin et al., 2020)										-0.2				
HuBERT (Nemeskey, 2020)											+3.6			
LitLatBERT (Ulčar and Robnik-Šikonja, 2021)												+2.7		
HerBERT (Mroczkowski et al., 2021)													+1.6	
RuBERT (Kuratov and Arkhipov, 2019)														+0.2
XLM-R large individual	+4.0	+4.6	+3.1	+4.1	+0.0	+6.9	+1.0	**+7.8**	+3.8	+3.3	+7.4	-0.8	+5.8	+4.8
RemBERT individual	-0.0	+4.9	+3.1	+3.1	-15.2	+0.0	+2.6	-18.3	+3.9	+3.8	+3.3	-4.3	+5.0	+4.3
XLM-R large multilingual	+6.1	**+6.1**	+2.1	+3.2	+8.0	**+16.2**	+4.1	+7.7	+5.0	+4.8	+6.9	**+4.6**	+5.1	+6.9
RemBERT multilingual	**+6.6**	+6.0	**+3.6**	**+4.4**	**+10.6**	+14.5	**+4.3**	+6.1	**+5.5**	**+5.1**	**+7.7**	+3.5	**+6.0**	**+9.0**
H) Effect of the Right Context Size; Development Version														
Right context 0	67.4	**70.7**	75.0	73.6	59.2	62.4	**68.3**	68.6	**74.4**	61.1	59.2	71.5	69.2	62.2
Right context 50	**+0.8**	-0.4	+1.3	+0.6	+3.9	+1.8	-0.7	**+1.2**	-0.5	+0.0	+1.7	**+0.5**	+0.3	**+1.7**
Right context 100	+0.6	-1.2	**+1.5**	**+0.7**	**+5.1**	**+2.7**	-0.1	-3.8	-0.5	**+0.6**	**+2.1**	-0.2	**+0.6**	+0.7
I) Effect of the Maximum Number of Links during Training; Development Version														
Unlimited	**67.4**	**70.7**	75.0	**73.6**	59.2	**62.4**	**68.3**	**68.6**	**74.4**	**61.1**	**59.2**	71.5	**69.2**	**62.2**
At most 1 link	-3.8	-3.3	-0.9	-3.6	-3.1	-4.3	-4.8	-8.7	-4.0	-3.1	-2.6	-5.0	-3.0	-3.8
At most 2 links	-1.4	-1.4	+0.2	-2.0	+1.5	-2.4	-1.9	-5.6	-0.8	-0.1	-1.0	-0.5	-2.6	-1.3
At most 3 links	-0.6	-0.9	**+0.5**	-0.2	**+3.5**	-0.4	-0.4	-6.5	-1.2	-0.4	-0.2	**+1.1**	-1.9	-0.6

Table 4: Ablation experiments evaluated on the development sets (CoNLL score in %). In A) and B), the scores of the official submissions are used; in C) to I), we report the highest development set score from any epoch.

4.7 Limiting Mention Spans to Their Heads

Comparison between full predicted mention spans and the predicted spans reduced to their syntactic heads in Table 4.A shows that *partial matching* favors post-processing which keeps syntactic heads and avoids "overprediction" beyond the gold mention span.

5 Conclusions

We presented a jointly trained pipeline approach as a winning contribution to the CRAC 2022 Shared Task on Multilingual Coreference Resolution (Žabokrtský et al., 2022). We published a thorough comparison of pretrained large language models for the task. Finally, we focused on multilingual models and we conclude that one multilingual, all-data model with large encoder outperformed individual monolingual fine-tuned models on all datasets. The source code is available at `https://github.com/ufal/crac2022-corpipe`.

Acknowledgements

This work has been supported by the Grant Agency of the Czech Republic, project EXPRO LUSyD (GX20-16819X), and has been using data provided by the LINDAT/CLARIAH-CZ Research Infrastructure (`https://lindat.cz`) of the Ministry of Education, Youth and Sports of the Czech Republic (Project No. LM2018101).

References

Jordi Armengol-Estapé, Casimiro Pio Carrino, Carlos Rodriguez-Penagos, Ona de Gibert Bonet, Carme Armentano-Oller, Aitor Gonzalez-Agirre, Maite Melero, and Marta Villegas. 2021. Are multilingual models the best choice for moderately underresourced languages? A comprehensive assessment for Catalan. In *Findings of the Association for Computational Linguistics: ACL-IJCNLP 2021*, pages 4933–4946, Online. Association for Computational Linguistics.

José Cañete, Gabriel Chaperon, Rodrigo Fuentes, Jou-Hui Ho, Hojin Kang, and Jorge Pérez. 2020. Spanish pre-trained bert model and evaluation data. In *PML4DC at ICLR 2020*.

Branden Chan, Stefan Schweter, and Timo Möller. 2020. German's next language model. In *Proceedings of the 28th International Conference on Computational Linguistics*, pages 6788–6796, Barcelona, Spain (Online). International Committee on Computational Linguistics.

Hyung Won Chung, Thibault Fevry, Henry Tsai, Melvin Johnson, and Sebastian Ruder. 2021. Rethinking embedding coupling in pre-trained language models. In *International Conference on Learning Representations*.

Alexis Conneau, Kartikay Khandelwal, Naman Goyal, Vishrav Chaudhary, Guillaume Wenzek, Francisco Guzmán, Edouard Grave, Myle Ott, Luke Zettlemoyer, and Veselin Stoyanov. 2020. Unsupervised cross-lingual representation learning at scale. In *Proceedings of the 58th Annual Meeting of the Association for Computational Linguistics*, pages 8440–8451, Online. Association for Computational Linguistics.

Jacob Devlin, Ming-Wei Chang, Kenton Lee, and Kristina Toutanova. 2019. BERT: Pre-training of deep bidirectional transformers for language understanding. In *Proceedings of the 2019 Conference of the North American Chapter of the Association for Computational Linguistics: Human Language Technologies, Volume 1 (Long and Short Papers)*, pages 4171–4186, Minneapolis, Minnesota. Association for Computational Linguistics.

Hongliang Fei, Xu Li, Dingcheng Li, and Ping Li. 2019. End-to-end deep reinforcement learning based coreference resolution. In *Proceedings of the 57th Annual Meeting of the Association for Computational Linguistics*, pages 660–665, Florence, Italy. Association for Computational Linguistics.

Mandar Joshi, Danqi Chen, Yinhan Liu, Daniel S. Weld, Luke Zettlemoyer, and Omer Levy. 2020. SpanBERT: Improving pre-training by representing and predicting spans. *Transactions of the Association for Computational Linguistics*, 8:64–77.

Mandar Joshi, Omer Levy, Luke Zettlemoyer, and Daniel Weld. 2019. BERT for coreference resolution: Baselines and analysis. In *Proceedings of the 2019 Conference on Empirical Methods in Natural Language Processing and the 9th International Joint Conference on Natural Language Processing (EMNLP-IJCNLP)*, pages 5803–5808, Hong Kong, China. Association for Computational Linguistics.

Ben Kantor and Amir Globerson. 2019. Coreference resolution with entity equalization. In *Proceedings of the 57th Annual Meeting of the Association for Computational Linguistics*, pages 673–677, Florence, Italy. Association for Computational Linguistics.

Diederik P. Kingma and Jimmy Ba. 2015. Adam: A method for stochastic optimization. In *ICLR (Poster), CoRR abs/1412.6980*.

Yuri Kuratov and Mikhail Y. Arkhipov. 2019. Adaptation of deep bidirectional multilingual transformers for russian language. *CoRR*, abs/1905.07213.

Kenton Lee, Luheng He, Mike Lewis, and Luke Zettlemoyer. 2017. End-to-end neural coreference resolution. In *Proceedings of the 2017 Conference on*

Empirical Methods in Natural Language Processing, pages 188–197, Copenhagen, Denmark. Association for Computational Linguistics.

Kenton Lee, Luheng He, and Luke Zettlemoyer. 2018. Higher-order coreference resolution with coarse-to-fine inference. In *Proceedings of the 2018 Conference of the North American Chapter of the Association for Computational Linguistics: Human Language Technologies, Volume 2 (Short Papers)*, pages 687–692, New Orleans, Louisiana. Association for Computational Linguistics.

Louis Martin, Benjamin Muller, Pedro Javier Ortiz Suárez, Yoann Dupont, Laurent Romary, Éric de la Clergerie, Djamé Seddah, and Benoît Sagot. 2020. CamemBERT: a tasty French language model. In *Proceedings of the 58th Annual Meeting of the Association for Computational Linguistics*, pages 7203–7219, Online. Association for Computational Linguistics.

Robert Mroczkowski, Piotr Rybak, Alina Wróblewska, and Ireneusz Gawlik. 2021. HerBERT: Efficiently pretrained transformer-based language model for Polish. In *Proceedings of the 8th Workshop on Balto-Slavic Natural Language Processing*, pages 1–10, Kiyv, Ukraine. Association for Computational Linguistics.

Anna Nedoluzhko, Michal Novák, Martin Popel, Zdeněk Žabokrtský, Amir Zeldes, Daniel Zeman, Peter Bourgonje, Silvie Cinková, Jan Hajič, Christian Hardmeier, Pauline Krielke, Frédéric Landragin, Ekaterina Lapshinova-Koltunski, M. Antònia Martí, Marie Mikulová, Maciej Ogrodniczuk, Marta Recasens, Manfred Stede, Milan Straka, Svetlana Toldova, Veronika Vincze, and Voldemaras Žitkus. 2022. Coreference in universal dependencies 1.0 (CorefUD 1.0). LINDAT/CLARIAH-CZ digital library at the Institute of Formal and Applied Linguistics (ÚFAL), Faculty of Mathematics and Physics, Charles University.

Anna Nedoluzhko, Michal Novák, Martin Popel, Zdeněk Žabokrtský, and Daniel Zeman. 2021. Coreference in universal dependencies 0.1 (CorefUD 0.1). LINDAT/CLARIAH-CZ digital library at the Institute of Formal and Applied Linguistics (ÚFAL), Faculty of Mathematics and Physics, Charles University.

Dávid Márk Nemeskey. 2020. *Natural Language Processing Methods for Language Modeling*. Ph.D. thesis, Eötvös Loránd University.

Ondřej Pražák, Miloslav Konopík, and Jakub Sido. 2021. Multilingual coreference resolution with harmonized annotations. In *Proceedings of the International Conference on Recent Advances in Natural Language Processing (RANLP 2021)*, pages 1119–1123.

Ondřej Pražák and Miloslav Konopik. 2022. End-to-end Multilingual Coreference Resolution with Mention Head Prediction. In *Proceedings of the CRAC 2022 Shared Task on Multilingual Coreference Resolution*. Association for Computational Linguistics.

Milan Straka, Jakub Náplava, Jana Straková, and David Samuel. 2021. Robeczech: Czech roberta, a monolingual contextualized language representation model. In *24th International Conference on Text, Speech and Dialogue*, pages 197–209, Cham, Switzerland. Springer.

Matej Ulčar and Marko Robnik-Šikonja. 2021. Training dataset and dictionary sizes matter in bert models: the case of baltic languages.

Ashish Vaswani, Noam Shazeer, Niki Parmar, Jakob Uszkoreit, Llion Jones, Aidan N Gomez, Ł ukasz Kaiser, and Illia Polosukhin. 2017. Attention is all you need. In *Advances in Neural Information Processing Systems*, volume 30. Curran Associates, Inc.

Liyan Xu and Jinho D. Choi. 2020. Revealing the myth of higher-order inference in coreference resolution. In *Proceedings of the 2020 Conference on Empirical Methods in Natural Language Processing (EMNLP)*, pages 8527–8533, Online. Association for Computational Linguistics.

Zdeněk Žabokrtský, Miloslav Konopík, Anna Nedoluzhko, Michal Novák, Maciej Ogrodniczuk, Martin Popel, Ondřej Pražák, Jakub Sido, Daniel Zeman, and Yilun Zhu. 2022. Findings of the Shared Task on Multilingual Coreference Resolution. In *Proceedings of the CRAC 2022 Shared Task on Multilingual Coreference Resolution*. Association for Computational Linguistics.

Author Index